Simply Ramen

A Complete Course in Preparing Ramen Meals at Home

Amy Kimoto-Kahn

Creator of easypeasyjapanesey.com

Race Point
PUBLISHING

Quarto is the authority on a wide range of topics.

Quarto educates, entertains and enriches the lives of our readers—enthusiasts and lovers of hands-on living.

www.quartoknows.com

First published in the United States of America in 2016 by
Race Point Publishing, a member of
Quarto Publishing Group USA Inc.
142 West 36th Street, 4th Floor
New York, NY 10018
www.quartoknows.com

10 9 8 7 6 5 4 3

ISBN: 978-1-63106-144-8

Names: Kimoto-Kahn, Amy, 1973- author.
Title: Simply ramen : a complete course in preparing Ramen meals at home / by
   Amy Kimoto-Kahn.
Description: New York, New York : Race Point Publishing, a member of Quarto
   Publishing Group USA Inc., [2015] | Includes index.
Identifiers: LCCN 2015034328 | ISBN 9781631061448 (hardcover)
Subjects: LCSH: Ramen. | Make-ahead cooking. | LCGFT: Cookbooks.
Classification: LCC TX809.N65 K565 2015 | DDC 641.82/2--dc23 LC record available at
http://lccn.loc.gov/2015034328

Editorial Director: Jeannine Dillon
Managing Editor: Erin Canning
Art Director and Cover Design: Heidi North
Food Photography: Colin Cooke
Food Stylist: Glynis Cotton
Location Photography: Andi Hatch Photography

Printed in China

Contents

Preface

Anyone who knows me knows that I love food. When I was a kid, I used to pretend I had my own cooking show and would make mud pies decorated with flowers from the yard. I would set up a table and pretend there was a mirror above me (remember, that's how they used to show food on cooking shows?) and angle my creations at the camera for all to see. My sous chef would always be Ponch, from the show *CHIPS*. Why? Because he was a babe and who wouldn't want him as a sous chef? I continued this love of cooking in the real kitchen and my mom would show me all of her tricks, such as how to fold my fingers against the top of an onion when slicing and how to use my thumb to measure the water above the rice. "Just above your first knuckle!" she would say. And how to add a crumbled bouillon cube and a drizzle of sesame oil over steamed broccoli to give it flavor. Like all good Asian moms, whether or not we had a party for five or fifty, we'd always have enough food to feed anyone who might happen to drop by.

As I grew up and the time came when I could afford my own super-sharp knives, I went down the career path that college prepared me for and continued working in marketing. Cooking was just a hobby, and I had no formal schooling in it; I just loved food—eating it and sharing it. My friends would say that I should open my own restaurant and my response was always that it would never happen because I didn't like to cook for strangers. I put so much effort and love into my cooking and I didn't know how I could share that with someone I didn't know.

The social-media boom hit and I was right in there, working with clients and making things happen for them, but on the side, I kept my little blog of my journey to one day fulfill the dream of having a cookbook, calling it *easypeasyjapanesey*. Then I decided to take myself a bit more seriously and hunted down an editor, Laurel Leigh. I say "hunted" because I literally found her name in a bunch of Williams-Sonoma cookbooks that I liked and cold-called her. I told her what I was thinking of doing and she said she wasn't sure why she felt compelled to work with me but that I could be her sort of pro-bono account. Just like that, I had an editor. Slow-forward five years and we finished a proposal to submit to a publisher. She felt it was time to introduce me to Leslie Jonath, a wonderful book packager with Connected Dots Media. Leslie's contacts then led me to Race Point, my publisher, and to Jan Newberry, a wicked good editor who helped keep me on the right track.

When Jeannine Dillon, my editor at Race Point, asked me if I would do a cookbook on ramen, honestly, my first thought was, "I don't know if I can do this. Ramen, now that ain't easypeasyjapanesey. . .that's huge." Then my husband, Dave, encouraged me to go for it. He said he could hold us afloat for the year and that he would turn into "Superdad" with the kids to cover the evenings and weekends. The blessing in all of this is how much my kids just adore him. They all run to the door and give him a king's welcome every night he comes home from work, and my two-year-old daughter, Ellie, looks at him like he's just the best thing since mini marshmallows. Throughout the process, I struggled with having so many original-style recipes versus an entire cookbook of just traditional ramen soups. It went against the Japanese in me to work on so many things at once instead of concentrating on just a few.

Original-style ramen is a term used in Japan for ramen made with nontraditional ingredients. It wasn't until I went to Japan and met Tomaharu Shono, the owner of Mensho Ramen (and five other ramen-yas in Tokyo, as well as one in San Francisco), that I felt vindicated. He's a top ramen chef and the master of original-style ramen. He'll often make limited-edition ramen that eager customers patiently line up for, knowing that when the soup runs out, it's "too bad, so sad." He uses ingredients such as foie gras and soy milk; spices such as cinnamon, cumin, and fennel; and even makes a chocolate noodle. He told me that there are no rules to original-style ramen, just as long as you show integrity in how you pull it all together. I showed him some of my recipes and he gave me a thumbs-up. I couldn't wait to get home and get my creative cooking juices flowing.

Amy Kimoto-Kahn

Introduction

I am a *yonsei*—a fourth-generation Japanese-American. Simply put, my great-grandparents on both sides were born in Japan and were the first in my family to move to America. My parents and grandparents were both interned to concentration camps during World War II. My Great Uncle Joe Fujimoto, on my mom's side, fought in the 442nd—the only fighting unit in the U.S. Army composed entirely of those with Japanese ancestry, while their families were subject to internment. Crazy stuff. I grew up in Fullerton, California, with an older brother and sister in the heart of Orange County. Even though I went to Japanese school on Saturdays for over eight years and studied Japanese in college, I don't speak the language much, but that's pretty common among yonsei. I find it ironic that my parents were taken from their homes and put into camps because of their ethnicity when their generation was taught to be as American as they could be to fit in—neither of my parents has any audible accent. They understood Japanese better than they could speak it, so the language wasn't often spoken in our home. I had never even been to Japan before I wrote this book.

For most of my childhood, we ate spaghetti and meatballs more often than we ate Japanese food, but we always had Japanese rice in a cooker that kept it warm for days. I know all the yonsei out there can relate. To this day, pork chops with white fluffy rice is a favorite dish of mine. It's this melding of Japan and America that has shaped my perspective on ramen. I felt that if I didn't go to Japan and eat and see where ramen came from, and if I didn't try to learn how to make it from an expert ramen master, I wouldn't feel like I had enough knowledge to write this book.

Going to Tokyo and eating some of the best ramen and attending ramen school in Osaka was life-changing—not only for this cookbook but for me as a Japanese-American, and the ramen experiences helped me develop my basic recipes and tailor them so that they are better suited for home cooks.

Closer to home, my research began at the best ramen shops near where I live in Northern California. I learned the difference between a good bowl of ramen and a great one. Most important to me are first the texture of the noodles and then the umami factor of the soup. Since high-quality ingredients were a given, I sourced mine from farmers' markets, local grocers, and Asian and Japanese markets—looking for organic where possible. I also got creative with leftovers and ingredients from my pantry.

For reference, I turned to the church cookbooks my family collected over the years from both my father's Buddhist roots and my mother's Presbyterian side. I gathered ideas from favorite recipes that have been passed down over generations and from old, treasured, Japanese cookbooks that my Auntie Alice gave me. The way that I make ramen is not 100 percent traditional, but with a big family to feed, I've needed to adopt a more practical approach for making delicious meals with ingredients that are accessible to me.

In this book, you'll learn the basics of making the traditional ramen soup bases and well-known toppings, as well as my original-style versions. If you like your ramen spicy, prefer vegetarian options, or other variations, you'll find plenty of those recipes here along with special dishes, such as Chilled Cucumber Tsukemen (page 117), where noodles are served separately to be dipped into a refreshing cold broth, and a Spicy Pork Tantanmen (page 98) with a *mazamen*, or no-broth, version of Chinese Dan Dan noodles, made with a sauce of blended chili oil, chili pepper, and sesame pastes with Szechuan-numbing spices inspired by the best tantanmen I had in Tokyo. And there's a Kamo Matcha Ramen (page 129) topped with tea-and-soy-sauce smoked duck, sliced pear, cilantro, and a marinated half-cooked egg that spills its liquid gold into a matcha-infused Shio (salt-based) broth.

I suggest you approach ramen as a step-by-step process that needn't be done in one day, making the soup base, noodles, and some basic toppings ahead of time. When you're ready to eat, you'll be surprised at how quickly you can pull it together.

My goal is to give you a taste of ramen culture, encourage you to learn more, and inspire you to create your own versions of ramen. All of my recipes call for one of the four basic soup bases—Tonkotsu, Shio, Miso, and Shoyu—but almost all of them can be interchanged, so don't feel like you have to use the one I've specified. Most of the ingredients for the recipes can be found in grocery stores or at farmers' markets, with only a few key ingredients, such as *dashi* (Japanese stock) and *kombu* (kelp used for flavoring soup stocks), that you may need to seek out at an Asian market or order online.

This is your chance to make your grocery shopping a cultural adventure and take your kids to a nearby Japanese grocery store. You'll be surprised by the many types of miso, *nori* (seaweed), and *shoyu* (soy sauce) there are to choose from. At our house, we've started a tradition of "build your own ramen night," with one soup base that everyone likes and a selection of DIY toppings. That's how I see ramen—it's whatever makes you happy. With *Simply Ramen*, you can enjoy ramen your way.

How to Build a Bowl of Ramen

This is not a recipe but an exercise for how you would assemble a bowl of ramen after you have made one or more of the soup bases and some of the toppings. Once you are able to orchestrate the timing of your ingredients to deliver a proper bowl that has all of the elements working together, these skills can then be transferred to any bowl that you make going forward.

There's an art to preparing everything in advance to ensure that all components are cooked perfectly and at the right temperatures when serving. My advice for following my recipes is to look at the prep time at the top of each recipe and the To Make in Advance section to know which components need to be made ahead of time. If you have these ready, your actual prep time to put it all together will be fairly quick.

Follow these easy steps and you'll have a bowl that will make you (and others) smile and give you the satisfaction that you've done it all from scratch at home—something to be proud of for sure.

* *In addition to Ramen Toppings (page 17), there are a myriad of additional toppings and condiments for topping your bowls of ramen.*

  Toppings: negi (green onion), sweet corn, parsley, butter, onions, yuzu citrus, bean sprouts, spinach, ginger, Japanese mushrooms (shitake, kirurage), kamaboko (Japanese fish cake), and takana (spicy pickled mustard greens).

  Condiments: white pepper, shoyu (soy sauce), shichimi-togarashi (mixed chili pepper spice), chili paste, fresh garlic, vinegar, chili oil, sesame seeds, and curry powder.

1   Place a pot of water to boil for your noodles. When it comes to a boil, make sure you wait until you have your soup base heated and your toppings ready to go before you cook your noodles.

2   In a large pot, bring your base or your base and stock (depending on the soup base you're using) to a boil, then lower heat and let simmer until it's ready to serve. Right before serving, crank it back up to boil.

3   (Optional) Ladle some of the boiling noodle water into your ramen bowl(s) for a couple of minutes to warm them before plating. Return the water to the pot to return to a boil.

4   Boil the noodles—if fresh, boil for about 1 minute; if packaged, boil for about 2 minutes. As soon as the noodles are done, shake out all of the excess water and lay them gently into your warmed serving bowls by folding them on top of each other so they do not look messy. Be prepared to assemble the entire bowl and serve it as soon as your noodles come out of the water!

5   Pour piping hot soup over the noodles in each bowl. Place your ramen and additional toppings on top. You did it! Now sit down, savor the moment, and enjoy slurping it all away!

Ramen Soup Bases
and Noodles

ラーメンの基本　スープと麺

Miso Base

LEVEL 1

Serves up to 12

Prep time: 45 minutes

Winters in Hokkaido in northern Japan are severe and the comfort and warmth of a good Miso Ramen have made it a daily staple. The quality of the miso makes all the difference in this recipe, so shop around and taste a variety of miso to find one that will add more depth.

Here, I've made a super flavorful Miso Base, or *misodare*, that can be enjoyed any time. (Please see Rameducate Yourself on page 152 to learn about the three components of all ramen.) Store it in the refrigerator, and when needed, you can make individual servings or enough to feed your whole family—this base offers the convenience of a one-person portion or a meal for many, all according to the base-to-stock ratio (3 tablespoons Miso Base to 1 cup/235 ml chicken or vegetable stock). Whether you're taking it to work for lunch or preparing a family meal, it will be worth the labor because once you make it, it's practically instant to serve up later. The Miso Base can be refrigerated for up to a week or frozen for one month.

1 medium-sized carrot, peeled and cut into large dice

½ onion, peeled and cut into large dice

½ apple, cored, peeled and cut into large dice

1 celery stalk, cut into large dice

3 garlic cloves

½ cup (120 ml) bacon fat (recommended), ghee, or coconut oil

2 tbsp sesame oil, divided

1½ cups (340 g) ground pork

2 tsp fresh ground ginger

1 tsp sriracha

2 tbsp soy sauce

1 tsp kelp granules (optional but recommended)

1 tbsp apple cider vinegar

1 tsp salt

1 tbsp ground sesame seed paste or tahini

¾ cup (175 ml) Shiro miso (white miso, which is lighter and sweeter)

¾ cup (175 ml) Akamiso miso (red miso, which is darker and saltier)

Low-sodium chicken or vegetable stock—2 cups (475 ml) per serving based on the number of servings

1   Add the carrot, onion, apple, celery, and garlic to a food processor. Pulse into a fine chop. It is better to use a food processor but if you don't have one, finely chop these ingredients by hand.

2   Add the bacon fat and 1 tablespoon sesame oil to a large skillet over medium-high heat. Add the finely chopped fruit and vegetables and cook until onions are translucent and apple is tender, stirring occasionally, for 10–12 minutes. When done, turn heat down to medium-low.

3   Add your ground pork to the cooked vegetable mixture. Cook for about 8–10 minutes until the meat is no longer pink. Stir in the ginger, sriracha, soy sauce, kelp granules, apple cider vinegar, and salt. Incorporate well.

4   Return the entire mixture to the food processor and pulse until pork is finely ground. It is better to use a food processer, but if you don't have one, then use a potato masher or wooden spoon to break the mixture into very small pieces in the skillet.

5   Add the sesame seed paste and miso to the ground pork mixture and mix well. It should have the consistency of a thick paste. Your base is done.

6   Bring the Miso Base and chicken or vegetable stock to a boil (depending on the number of people you are serving, use the ratio of 3 tablespoons Miso Base to 1 cup (235 ml) chicken or vegetable stock). Lower heat and let simmer until it's ready to serve. Use about 2 cups (475 ml) soup per serving. Right before serving, crank the heat back up to boil the soup.

7   Pour 2 cups soup (475 ml) over each bowl of noodles. Top each bowl with desired toppings. (See How to Build a Bowl of Ramen on page xi for help with timing the orchestration of your ramen components.)

Tonkotsu Base

LEVEL 3

Serves 10

Prep time: 4 hours, plus time to make Chashu

Equipment: 30-quart pressure cooker (always read and follow the instructions provided with your pressure cooker before you start)

To Make in Advance

....

Chashu with its braising liquid (page 22)

....

The Tonkotsu Base is the holy grail of ramen soup bases, and this recipe follows the traditional recipe I learned to make from Sensei Miyajima Rikisai at the Miyajima Ramen School in Osaka, Japan. Tonkotsu, known as "white soup," comes from two different regions in Japan. This version comes from the Kanto region of Tokyo. It uses a double-soup method, where two separate broths are combined right before serving, making a more complex and flavorful soup.

Seabura (boiled pork back fat)

1½ lbs (700 g) pork back fat, cut into strips

Water, to cover

Tonkotsu Soup

½ lb (225 g) chicken feet, cleaned, extra skin removed and nails cut off (approximately 6 feet)

8–10 lbs (3.6–4.5 kg) pork knuckles/trotters, pounded with a mallet to release marrow

1 lb (455 g) potatoes, unpeeled and sliced in big chunks

5 qts (4.7 L) water

Shiodare (salt flavor component)

1 large rectangular piece kombu (about 10 inches/25 cm long), cut into large squares

1 large or 2 small dried shiitake mushrooms, crumbled

1 qt (946 ml) water

2 tbsp bonito flakes

1½ cups (300 g) baby clams

½ cup (140 g) table salt

Shoyudare (soy sauce flavor component)

Equal parts Shiodare and Chashu braising liquid (do not assemble until ready to use)

1. Before cooking, you must have the **Chashu with its braising liquid** on hand to use later.
2. Make the Seabura: Place the pork back fat in a large pot, cover with water, bring to a boil, and simmer for 4 hours, uncovered.
3. Make the Tonkotsu Soup: In a separate pot of boiling water, blanch the chicken feet, drain, and then add them to the pressure cooker along with the pork knuckles or trotters and the potatoes. Cover with up to 5 quarts (4.7 L) water, making sure the total volume of water and food combined does not exceed half of the pot.
4. Leave your pressure regulator weight off of the vent pipe. Turn heat to high until steam flows from the vent pipe (this may take up to 20 minutes) and continue to let vent for 10 minutes more while the steam displaces the air in the cooker. Maintain high heat setting and start timing your cooking when the regulator weight begins to jiggle or rock. It may appear as if it is leaking, but this is normal. Regulate the heat so that the weight only jiggles 1–4 times per minute. Start a timer and cook for 1 hour.
5. Make the Shiodare: In a medium-sized pot, bring the kombu, shiitake, and 4 cups (950 ml) water to a boil. Lower the heat and simmer for 5 minutes. Drain the kombu and shiitake and put the soup into a clean medium-sized pot.
6. Return this drained soup to the stove, add the bonito flakes, and heat to a boil, then simmer for 5 minutes. Drain the bonito flakes and put soup into your other empty pot, pressing the flakes to release all their liquid.
7. Return this drained soup to the stove and add the clams, bring to a boil, then simmer for 5 minutes. Remove the clams with a sieve and measure out 1 quart or 4 cups (1 L) soup into your other empty pot (you will have a minimal amount to discard). Whisk in ½ cup (140 g) table salt. Note that the salt to soup ratio should be 20 percent, resulting in a very salty soup base or **Shiodare**.
8. After 1 hour, take the pressure cooker off the heat and allow the pressure gauge to return to 0 (zero) before gently removing the cover. Push down the pork bones to get the bone fat out and make the soup creamier and thicker. Cook on a medium low heat with the cover off for about 1 hour longer, mixing periodically.
9. Directly into your serving bowls, add 1 tablespoon of your Chashu braising liquid and 1 tablespoon Shiodare per serving to make a **Shoyudare**.
10. Drain and remove the pork back fat that has been simmering. Cut the strips into smaller 2-inch (5 cm) pieces. Into a medium-sized bowl, take a large-holed sieve and push a couple of pieces at a time through the sieve so that you see it come through the other side in small little bits. Repeat until all pieces are pushed through. Your **Seabura** is ready. Set aside.
11. Strain all of the solids from the Tonkotsu soup in the pressure cooker and transfer the soup to a separate pot and keep warm. Right before serving, crank it up to a boil.

12 Remove the Chashu from its braising liquid and cut into ¼-inch (6mm) thick rounds. Sauté your sliced pork in a skillet for 1–2 minutes to render the fat and make the slices crispy before placing on top of ramen. Use as many slices as you'd like to serve on your ramen—typical amounts vary from 1–3 slices.

13 To assemble your bowl, add 1 cup (235 ml) piping hot Tonkotsu soup to your Shoyudare (Step 9) and 1 tablespoon of the Seabura (Step 10) to each serving portion, then add your noodles and place the sliced Chashu on top along with desired toppings. (See How to Build a Bowl of Ramen on page xi for help with timing the orchestration of your ramen components.)

Shoyu Base

LEVEL 2

Serves up to 12

Prep time: 8–10 hours,
plus 30 minutes
to strain

If you've made my Tonkotsu Base (page 5), then you have a basic *shoyudare*, or strong soy sauce flavor base, with which you can combine any stock or fat to make a simple shoyu ramen. This recipe combines the stock, shoyudare, and fat into one. (Please see Rameducate Yourself on page 152 to learn about the three components of all ramen.)

With this recipe, I've slow-cooked oxtail sections within my broth in a good crock pot, which helps render the fat from the bones without having to constantly stir. You could also make this in a slow cooker, large Dutch oven, or heavy-duty pot. The oxtail adds a meaty goodness and complexity to the fat component that complements the soy sauce. You'll have to go to an Asian market to find dashi, or Japanese stock, which comes in granular form—there are many varieties to choose from, so just make sure to pick one that has bonito fish as the primary ingredient. It's also important to have dried shiitake mushrooms, as they'll give a more intense flavor to the soup than fresh ones. The final soup will taste overly salty, but when the noodles are added in, they will soak up the sauce and balance it out.

4 tbsp bacon fat (recommended), ghee, or coconut oil
2 medium-sized carrots, peeled and cut into large dice
½ onion, peeled and cut into large dice
3 green onions, cut into thirds
1 apple, cored and quartered (with skin on)
2 celery stalks, cut into thirds
5 garlic cloves, peeled and left whole
5 dried shiitake mushrooms, broken up into small pieces
1 whole organic chicken
4 medium oxtail sections, roughly 2 inches (5 cm) long
1 lemon, quartered
2 qts (2.2 L) low-sodium chicken stock
¾ cup (175 ml) high-grade soy sauce
4 tsp dashi granules (Japanese stock)
2 tbsp salt
½ tsp white pepper
1 bay leaf

1. In a crock pot, slow cooker, large Dutch oven, or heavy-duty pot, combine the bacon fat, carrots, onion, green onions, apple, celery, garlic, and dried shiitake mushrooms.
2. Add the whole chicken, oxtails, and lemon, then pour over the chicken stock, followed by the soy sauce, dashi, salt, pepper, and bay leaf—the stock should almost cover the chicken.
3. Set the crock pot or slow cooker to high and let cook for 10 hours. If using a large Dutch oven or pot, bring to a boil over a high heat and set in an oven preheated to 200°F (90°C) for 8–10 hours. When the oxtail meat easily falls off the bone, your soup is done.
4. With a slotted spoon, remove all of the larger solids and discard. Strain the remaining solids with a finer sieve into a large pot. You should have a light brown, glossy, and fat-rich soup. At this point the stock can be refrigerated for up to 2 weeks or frozen for 1 month.
5. In a separate saucepan, bring the Shoyu Base to a boil, then lower the heat and let simmer until it's ready to serve. Use about 2 cups (475 ml) per serving. Right before serving, crank it back up to a boil.
6. Pour 2 cups soup (475 ml) over each bowl of noodles. Top each bowl with desired toppings. (See How to Build a Bowl of Ramen on page xi for help with timing the orchestration of your ramen components.)

Shio Base

If you've made my Tonkotsu Base (page 5), then you have a basic *shiodare*, or strong salt flavor base, with which you can combine any stock or fat to make a simple shio ramen. This recipe is a variation of shiodare but adds additional flavor so that you can simply combine it with a chicken or vegetable stock for a flavorful soup. (Please see Rameducate Yourself on page 152 to learn about the three components of all ramen.)

This recipe starts off with the same components as the Miso Base (page 3), but I've added fresh and dried shiitake mushrooms to give it added depth. It also incorporates the nice fatty flavor of bacon fat. I experimented with different types of salt for this recipe to see which came through the best; I chose fleur de sel because I like the earthiness that it adds without it being overwhelmingly salty, and it helps keep the taste of the soup lingering on the palate. You can make your own original recipe with any special salt you have on hand.

1 medium-sized carrot, peeled and chopped
½ onion, peeled and cut into large dice
3 green onions, white part only, chopped
½ apple, peeled, cored, and chopped
1 celery stalk, cut into large dice
3 garlic cloves
5 fresh shiitake mushrooms
½ cup (120 ml) bacon fat (recommended), ghee, or coconut milk
1 tbsp sesame oil
3 tsp dashi granules (Japanese stock)
2 tbsp fleur de sel or salt of your choice

Broth
Unsalted butter (2 tbsp per serving)
Low-sodium chicken or vegetable stock (2 cups/475 ml per serving)
Mirin (2 tbsp per serving)
1 large rectangular piece kombu (about 10 inches/25 cm long), cut into large squares
Dried shiitake mushrooms, crumbled (2 mushrooms per serving)

1. In a food processor, combine the carrot, onion, green onions, apple, celery, garlic, and fresh shiitake mushrooms and process until very finely chopped, almost like a paste. It is better to use a food processor, but if you don't have one, finely chop these ingredients by hand.

2. In a medium-sized pot, warm the bacon fat and sesame oil over medium-high heat. Add the finely chopped vegetables and cook, stirring occasionally, until the onions are translucent and the apple is tender, 10–12 minutes. Add the dashi and fleur de sel, and mix well.

3. To make the broth, add the butter to a large saucepan over medium-high heat. Once the butter starts to brown and smells nutty, add the stock, mirin, kombu, and mushrooms. Bring to a boil, reduce heat, and let simmer for at least 15 minutes, then remove solids with a sieve. Add the Shio Base to the broth (depending on the number of people you are serving, it's 3 tablespoons Shio Base to every 1 cup/235 ml broth). Lower heat and let simmer until it's ready to serve. Use about 2 cups (475 ml) soup per serving. Right before serving, crank the heat back up to boil.

4. Pour 2 cups (475 ml) soup over each bowl of noodles and add your desired toppings. (See How to Build a Bowl of Ramen on page xi for help with timing the orchestration of your ramen components.)

Ramen Noodles

LEVEL 3

Serves 8

Prep time: 3 hours

There's no getting around the fact that making every element of ramen from scratch is a lot of work. The good news is that almost all the components—the fat; the *tare*, or highly flavored season component; the broth; the toppings; and the noodles—can be made over the course of several days. If you make these ahead of time, then when you're ready to assemble your ramen, it can be done relatively quickly. These noodles can be wrapped in individual portions and frozen for up to one month. You will need a pasta machine, and I'd recommend using an electric mixer with a dough hook, unless you want to develop Popeye forearms....

Remember, there are lots of other, easier noodle alternatives that are perfectly fine. Any of the following will work, just throw out those salty flavor packets:

- fresh noodles from a ramen shop
- fresh packaged noodles that come with a soup-base packet
- dried ramen noodles for instant ramen
- dried chuka soba noodles (*chuka soba* actually translates to "Chinese noodle," which are, in fact, ramen noodles)
- gluten-free packaged ramen noodles or rice ramen noodles for dietary restrictions

If you do venture down the homemade noodle path, then keep this in mind: a perfect noodle has a yellow hue, should be cooked al dente, and have a chewy and elastic, yet firm texture that holds up to the soup without getting soggy, all the way until the very last slurp.

2 tsp "baked baking soda" (recipe on page 14) or kansui powder

1¼ cups (295 ml) water (if you are hand-kneading, change water quantity to 1½ cups, or 355 ml)

3½ cups (490 g) bread flour, plus extra for dusting

½ cup (60 g) cake flour

1 cup (150 g) wheat flour

1 tbsp salt

Cornstarch, for dusting

1. In a small bowl, combine the baked baking soda or kansui powder and water until it dissolves.
2. In a stand mixer fitted with a dough hook, combine the bread, cake, and wheat flours, kansui water, and salt. Mix for 10 minutes on the lowest speed until the dough forms little pellets. If you need to, add up to 5 additional teaspoons of water. The dough is ready when it still feels dry but comes together when squeezed with your hand.
3. Tip the dough onto a floured board and knead into a ball for at least 10 minutes. Alternatively, you can put your dough in a plastic zip-top bag and form it into a ball so that it is easier to bring together and knead.
4. When you are ready to make your pasta, set up your pasta machine so that it is stable and won't slip from your work surface.
5. Cut your dough ball into 8 equal-sized pieces and use one piece at a time, keeping the rest wrapped tightly with plastic wrap or sealed in your zip-top bag and refrigerated.
6. Roll out one piece until it resembles a flat, long shape. Sprinkle with some cornstarch so it doesn't stick to the pasta maker. Pass it through your pasta maker on the largest setting—it will be a bit rough at the edges, but don't worry about how it looks. Fold it over on itself and pass it through the machine again.
7. Reduce the machine width to 2 and pass through. Fold it over on itself and pass it through again.
8. Reduce the machine width to 4 and pass it through only once. You will now have one long strip of dough. Cut this strip in half vertically.
9. Reduce the machine width to 6 and pass through one of the halves twice. Repeat with the other half. Now your dough is ready to run through the noodle cutter attachment.
10. The two strips will yield enough noodles for 1 bowl of ramen. Repeat steps 6–8 for the remaining dough pieces from step 5. Sprinkle each batch of noodles with additional cornstarch, lifting up the noodles to separate and lightly coat them, then pack them individually in plastic wrap. Let them sit in the refrigerator for at least a day before using. If you are planning to use them later, put them in individual ziplock bags and store them in the freezer for up to one month.
11. Cook the fresh pasta in a pot of boiling water. Depending on the number of portions, cook for 1–2 minutes. Shake out all excess water and lay a portion in your bowl of hot soup by folding them over onto each other so they do not look messy. Then add the soup and toppings.

How to Make "Baked Baking Soda"

Baked baking soda replaces a Japanese ingredient known as *kansui* that is often difficult to find and that gives ramen noodles their signature yellow hue and firmness. Harold McGee, the king of kitchen science, discovered that by baking baking soda, you could get the same effect as the kansui. Spread 1/4 cup (55 g) baking soda on a foil-lined baking sheet and place it in an oven preheated to 275°F (135°C) for 1 hour. As this recipe only calls for 2 teaspoons, you can save the remainder in a zip-top bag. Just fold up the baking soda in the foil to make it easier to put in a storage bag.

Ramen Toppings

ラーメントッピング

Tamagoyaki (Japanese Omelet)

LEVEL 2

**Makes enough for
4 ramen portions**

Prep time: 10 minutes

You will need a Japanese *tamagoyaki* frying pan (it's rectangular) to get a visually appealing omelet. If you don't have one, a regular frying pan will work, but you won't end up with the uniform rectangular shape that distinguishes this omelet.

3 eggs
1 green onion, chopped
1 tsp shoyu (soy sauce)
1 tsp sugar
1/4 tsp salt
Nonstick cooking spray

1   In a medium-sized bowl, whisk the eggs with the green onion, shoyu, sugar, and salt until foamy.
2   Over medium-high heat, warm 1 teaspoon vegetable oil in a frying pan. Drip a tiny bit of egg in the pan—if it sizzles on contact, the pan is sufficiently hot. Add about a quarter of the egg mixture to the pan and tilt the pan so that the egg mixture covers the bottom in a thin, even layer. The egg will start cooking quickly so you'll need to move fast.
3   Using chopsticks, gently roll the egg mixture tightly toward you from the part of the pan farthest from the handle.
4   Quickly add a little more cooking spray to the exposed part of the pan.
5   Pour another quarter of the egg mixture into the pan, lifting up the cooked portion to get some egg mixture underneath it to cook.
6   Roll the egg mixture away from you this time as it combines and attaches to the cooked egg layer. Nudge it to the back to the front of the pan, where you started before.
7   Repeat two more times until you've used all of the egg—the omelet will obviously increase in size with each layer.
8   Roll the omelet out of the pan and you should have a rectangular-shaped block with your layers of egg. Let cool and slice vertically before serving.

Menma (Seasoned Bamboo Shoots)

LEVEL 1

Serves 12

Prep time: 30 minutes

This is a popular topping for ramen, and there is a world of difference between fresh bamboo shoots and canned. If you can't find fresh bamboo, I would forgo using it entirely. You can find fresh bamboo in most Asian grocery stores; you can recognize it by its signature conical shape.

1 lb (455 g) fresh bamboo shoots
1 tbsp sesame oil
2 cups (475 ml) water
3 tsp dashi granules
1 tbsp shoyu (soy sauce)
1 tbsp sake
2 tsp sugar
1 tsp salt

1 Cut the bamboo shoots in half lengthwise and then into thin slices horizontally.
2 In a large sauté pan over medium-high heat, combine the sesame oil, water, dashi, shoyu, sake, sugar, and salt. Add the bamboo shoots.
3 Heat, uncovered, until the bamboo has absorbed most of the liquid, about 20 minutes. Remove from heat and store in an airtight container. Will keep for up to one week in the refrigerator or frozen for up to 1 month.

Poached Eggs

LEVEL 1

Makes as many eggs as you need

Prep time: 10 minutes

Poached eggs aren't as labor-intensive as Marinated Half-Cooked Eggs (page 26), and their runny center provides an instant sauce to swirl into ramen soup. Cook them ahead of time and when your other ramen components are ready to assemble, just warm the poached eggs in the ramen cooking water for 10 seconds before gently transferring to the bowls.

Dash of white vinegar or squeeze of lemon juice
Eggs (as many as you need)

1 Fill a medium-sized pot with about 1½ inches (3.5 cm) water and bring to a boil over high heat. Add the white vinegar or lemon juice—this will help the eggs to coagulate quicker and reduce the amount of feathering around the edges, but don't add too much or the eggs will taste sour. Once the water comes to a boil, reduce to just above a simmer.
2 Crack an egg into a small ramekin or cup. If poaching more than one egg, prepare up to 3 ramekins at a time—I don't recommend cooking more than 3 at a time.
3 Gently slide the eggs out of the ramekins and into the simmering water. Take care not to crowd the pan.
4 Cook the eggs until the whites are opaque, about 3½ minutes.
5 With a slotted spoon, transfer the cooked eggs to a paper towel to drain. If not using immediately, store in a water bath in an airtight container and refrigerate for up to 2 days.

Chashu (Braised Pork)

LEVEL 2

Serves 4-6, based on 3 slices per serving

Prep time: 4 hours cooking time

Chashu is one of the most popular ramen toppings. It can vary in flavor, size, and fat content—one ramen-ya might serve three thick, juicy pieces; another might give you two wafer-thin slices the size of half your bowl. Its origin, just like ramen, stems from the Chinese *char-siu*, roasted or barbecued pork. You may recognize char-siu by its signature red exterior and lean meat, but Japanese chashu is completely different. It's not red, has more fat and tenderness, and is typically braised rather than barbecued. Braising calls for cooking it in liquid at low heat until the tough collagen in the meat breaks down. The result is a melt-in-your mouth experience. Chashu can be made from different cuts of pork and is traditionally tied so that it can be sliced into rounds.

2-lb (900 g) slab of pork shoulder or other part with fat, cut into 4–5 inch (10–13 cm) wide pieces, rolled up into a nice round bundle, and tightly trussed with cooking string to keep its shape

2½ qts or 10 cups (2.8 L) water

1 qt or 4¼ cups (946 ml) dark shoyu (soy sauce)

2½ cups (500 g) sugar

¾ cup (175 ml) mirin (sweet rice wine)

1 green onion, chopped

1 tbsp grated ginger

1 Combine the pork with the water, shoyu, sugar, mirin, onion, and ginger in a large pot over high heat. Bring to a boil, reduce to a simmer and cook until the pork is tender, about 4 hours. Skim off any scum that floats to the surface.

2 Remove the pork from the liquid. Insert a medium-thick wooden skewer into the center of the meat. If it comes out clean, the pork is done.

3 When you are ready to use it, take the pork out of the liquid. Save the liquid for Marinated Half-Cooked Eggs (page 26) or adding to your Shoyu Ramen Base—do not throw this away! Let the pork rest for at least 2 hours or overnight in the braising liquid in the refrigerator to make it easier to slice—overnight is best as the pork will continue to soak up the juices in that time.

4 Sauté your sliced pork in a skillet for 1–2 minutes to render the fat and make the slices crispy before placing on top of ramen. Cut into ¼ inch (6 mm) thick rounds. Use as many slices as you'd like to serve on your ramen—typical amounts vary from 1–3 slices.

Roasted Nori (Seaweed)

LEVEL 1

Makes 2 squares per portion

Prep time: 2 minutes

These days you can find roasted and flavored seaweed in grocery stores, coffee shops, and even vending machines. I prefer to roast my own because some of the varieties out there are too oily or aren't crunchy enough for me. If you purchase a pack of seaweed made for sushi in big sheets, you can roast them over an open gas flame in seconds. (Unfortunately, this can't be done on an electric stove.) If you do it this way, I promise you'll never go back to buying ready-roasted seaweed. It's far tastier and crisper when you make it yourself.

Japanese nori (seaweed) in sheets
Nonstick cooking spray or sesame oil
Sea salt or kosher salt

1 Spray both sides of each sheet of seaweed with cooking spray or wipe sesame oil over it using a folded paper towel.
2 Over a low flame on a gas stove, gently waft the seaweed back and forth on both sides until crisp.
3 Set the finished roasted seaweed sheet on a paper towel and repeat with additional sheets.
4 Sprinkle each sheet with salt and stack them about 4 or 5 high.
5 Cut each stack into quarters with a sharp chef's knife or with kitchen shears.

Beni Shoga (Pickled Ginger)

LEVEL 1

Serves 30

Prep time: 2 weeks

Most recipes for *beni shoga* call for fresh shiso, but since store-bought umeboshi vinegars tend to have shiso leaves in their liquid, I forgo using fresh shiso. What's great is you can use the leftover umeboshi brine to complement any salad. This recipe is from a variation of the brine I use for bread and butter pickles. I love its sweet and sour balance with the subtleness of the sugar and extra zing from mustard seeds.

6 oz (170 g) fresh ginger root (about 3 medium-sized stalks)

1 cup (235 ml) umeboshi (pickled Japanese plum) vinegar *

2 tbsp salt

4 tbsp sugar

4 tbsp mirin (sweet rice wine)

1 tsp yellow mustard seeds

* *you can purchase umeboshi vinegar at an Asian grocery store or online*

1 Peel the ginger and cut into ¼-inch (6 mm) slices.
2 In a small jar, combine the umeboshi vinegar, salt, sugar, mirin, and mustard seeds. Cover and shake to combine.
3 Add the ginger to the jar, cover, and refrigerate for 2 weeks.
4 Remove the ginger slices from the brine and julienne into thin strips.

Ajitsuke Tamago
(Marinated Half-Cooked Egg)

LEVEL 2

**Makes 6 eggs and
2 cups (450 ml)
teriyaki sauce**

**Prep time: 1½ hours,
plus 2 days to
marinate**

I try to save time when it comes to cooking in my house, so this recipe is actually two. The ingredients I use to soak my half-cooked eggs in are the same as my mom's recipe for teriyaki sauce. If you want to skip the teriyaki sauce step entirely, that's fine, too. The other short cut: if you are making or plan to make Chashu (page 22) or Kakuni (page 28), you can use the braising liquid left over from that recipe to soak your eggs.

1 cup (235 ml) shoyu (soy sauce)
1 cup (200 g) sugar
1½ tsp grated ginger
1 tsp minced garlic
½ cup (120 ml) mirin (sweet rice wine)
6 eggs, at room temperature*
½ cup bonito fish flakes

*   *Eggs should be brought to an even temperature in a warm bath before boiling so that cooking times do not vary. Also, poke a pin-sized hole in the bottom of the shells of the eggs for easy peeling later.*

1. In a medium saucepan over high heat, whisk together the shoyu, sugar, ginger, and garlic in a medium saucepan. Once the mixture starts bubbling and the sugar dissolves, remove from the heat. Make sure it doesn't bubble over. Stir in the mirin and cool to room temperature or refrigerate for at least 1 hour.

2. Bring a large pot of water to a boil. With a slotted spoon or a Chinese strainer, gently add the eggs to the boiling water, and immediately set a timer for 6½ minutes.

3. While the eggs are cooking, prepare an ice-bath for them. When the eggs are done, immediately transfer them to the ice bath. Let them cool in the ice bath for about 10 minutes, then remove the eggs and peel them.

4. In a shallow container that is deep enough for the eggs to be covered in liquid, combine 3 cups (700 ml) water and 1 cup (235 ml) teriyaki sauce, or 1 cup (235 ml) Chashu liquid (see page 22). Add your eggs; cover them with a paper towel by pressing the paper towel down so it's touching the top of the eggs; and pour the bonito fish flakes over the paper towel—the weight of the paper towel will help the eggs marinate on all sides and the bonito flakes will flavor the eggs. Let marinate in the refrigerator for 2 days.

5. Remove the eggs from their soaking liquid and cut each one in half with a very sharp knife. You'll end up with a beautiful half-cooked egg filled with liquid-gold goodness, ready to complete any ramen recipe!

Kakuni (Braised Pork Belly)

LEVEL 2

**Serves 4–6, based on
3 slices per serving**

**Prep time: 4 hours
cooking time**

Kakuni is a pork ramen topping, but it literally means "square simmered." It's cooked in a fashion similar to Chashu (page 22) but the pork is cut into squares before it is braised. When making kakuni, save the reserved braising liquid. It is a useful ingredient for Marinated Half-Cooked Eggs (page 26), or for combining with shiodare to make a very basic Shoyu Base (page 8).

1 lb (455 g) boneless pork belly, cut into large
   squares
2½ qts or 10 cups (2.8 L) water
1 qt or 4¼ cups (946 ml) dark shoyu (soy sauce)
2½ cups (500 g) sugar
¾ cup (175 ml) mirin (sweet rice wine)
1 garlic clove
1 green onion, chopped
1 tbsp grated ginger

1   Combine the pork with the water, shoyu, sugar, mirin, garlic, onion, and ginger in a large pot over high heat. Bring to a boil, reduce to a simmer and cook until the pork is tender, about 4 hours. Skim off any scum that floats to the surface.

2   Remove the pork from the liquid. Insert a medium-thick wooden skewer into the center of the meat. If it comes out clean, the pork is done.

3   When you are ready to use it, take the pork out of the liquid. Save the liquid for Marinated Half-Cooked Eggs (page 26) or for adding to your Shoyu Base (page 8)—do not throw this away! Let the pork rest for at least 2 hours or overnight in the braising liquid in the refrigerator to make it easier to slice—overnight is best as the pork will continue to soak up the juices in that time.

4   Saute your sliced pork in a skillet for 1–2 minutes to render the fat and make the slices crispy before placing on top of ramen. Cut into smaller cubes. Use as many cubes as you'd like to serve on your ramen—typical amounts vary from 1–3 pieces.

Mayu (Black Garlic Oil)

LEVEL 2

Makes ½ cup (120 ml), enough for 12 servings

Prep time: 10 minutes

Mayu is often used to add depth and flavor to ramen. It's very bitter on its own but mixes well when used in small quantities. Because this recipe requires cooking the garlic until it's charred and completely blackened, I use avocado oil for its high smoke point. Store in a plastic squeeze bottle and drizzle a small amount over the top of the ramen soup before serving.

¼ cup (60 ml) avocado oil
8 garlic cloves, minced
¼ cup (60 ml) sesame oil

1 In a small saucepan over high heat, warm the avocado oil for about 2 minutes. Add the garlic and stir until it turns dark brown. Reduce the heat to medium and continue stirring occasionally until the garlic blackens.

2 Transfer the mixture to a blender and add the sesame oil. Blend on high until well incorporated and smooth.

Roasted Garlic Butter

LEVEL 2

Serves 4, based on
1 tablespoon portions

Prep time:
1 hour, 15 minutes

Many ramen shops offer fresh garlic cloves and a press at the table so you can squeeze the garlic right into your ramen. I prefer the subtler flavor of roasted garlic (plus I don't like sweating garlic all day!). This butter adds flavor and richness to any ramen soup. It's also delicious as a spread on bread or toast.

1 garlic bulb
Salt and pepper, to season
Olive oil, for drizzling
¼ cup or ½ stick (55 g) unsalted butter,
    at room temperature

1 Preheat the oven to 400°F (200°C).
2 Cut about ¼-inch (6 mm) off the top of the garlic bulb to expose the tips of the cloves and place the garlic on a piece of aluminum foil.
3 Drizzle the bulb with olive oil, season with salt and pepper, and wrap with the foil to cover completely.
4 Place the wrapped garlic on a cookie sheet. Bake on the center rack for 1 hour, until the bulb starts popping out of its skin and is caramel in color. Feel free to peek in the oven to check.
5 Remove from the oven and let cool for 15 minutes. Break apart the bulb and squeeze the garlic cloves out of their skins onto a cutting board. With the back of a knife or a fork, mash the cloves into a paste.
6 Transfer to a small bowl and combine with the butter until well incorporated. Store in an airtight container and refrigerate for up to 4 weeks. Bring to room temperature before using.

Garlic Chips

LEVEL 1

Serves 10 or less, depending on how much you want to add

Prep time: 8 minutes

These little flavored chips add just the right texture and balance to the ramen soup. They don't stay crisp for long, though, so prepare them just before you need them.

Extra virgin olive oil, for frying
5 garlic cloves, thinly sliced

1 Fill a small saucepan with about ½-inch (1.25 cm) olive oil and set over medium-high heat. Line a plate with a paper towel.
2 Add a single garlic slice to the hot oil. If it sizzles on contact, you're ready to begin cooking. Add the garlic slices in 2 batches and cook just until lightly browned, 5–8 seconds. Watch carefully—these cook very fast and need to be removed promptly, or they will burn and taste very bitter.
3 With a slotted spoon, transfer the cooked garlic chips to the paper towel–lined plate and let cool before serving.

Fried Onions

LEVEL 1

Makes 8 portions, using a healthy pile per portion

Prep time: 10 minutes

These delicate fried onions add crunch and texture to a bowl of ramen and stay crisp even when soaking in the soup. Just try not to eat them all before you sit down to eat! These are best when eaten immediately after frying, but they can be stored in an airtight container and reheated in a toaster oven.

2 cups (475 ml) vegetable oil, for frying

1 red onion, halved and thinly sliced, preferably
  with a mandoline

Salt, to season

1   Fill a large a large heavy-duty frying pan with ½-inch (1.25 cm) oil and set over medium heat. Line a plate with a paper towel.

2   Add an onion slice to the hot oil. If it sizzles on contact, you're ready to fry. Add small batches of onions to the hot oil, taking care that they don't form clumps. Cook until browned and crisp, about 15 seconds. Watch closely—these can burn quickly.

3   With a slotted spoon, transfer the onions to the paper towel–lined plate to cool. Repeat with the remaining batches.

4   Lightly season with salt.

Fried String Potatoes

LEVEL 1

Makes 8 portions, using a healthy pile per portion

Prep time: 10 minutes

Called *pommes pailles* by the French, these make a delicious topping for ramen. Unlike regular fried potatoes, they stay crisp for hours and you can keep them for up to 3 days—store them in an airtight container and re-crisp them in a toaster oven before use.

2 cups (475 ml) vegetable oil, for frying

1 russet potato, skin on, thinly sliced, preferably with a mandoline

Salt, to season

1 Fill a large heavy-duty frying pan with ½-inch (1.25 cm) oil and set over medium-high heat. Line a plate with a paper towel.

2 Add a potato strip to the hot oil. If it sizzles on contact, you're ready to fry. Add small batches of potatoes to the hot oil and cook until browned and crisp, about 15 seconds. Watch closely—these can burn quickly.

3 With a slotted spoon, transfer the crisped potatoes to the paper-towel-lined plate to cool. Repeat with the remaining batches.

4 Lightly season with salt.

Miso Butter

LEVEL 1

Red miso paste tends to be a bit saltier than white, which is why I prefer it for this miso butter. It delivers more of a kick.

Serves 4, based on 1 tablespoon portions

Prep time: 5 minutes

¼ cup or ½ stick (55 g) unsalted butter, at room temperature

3 tsp red miso paste

1 In a small bowl, combine the butter and miso paste with a spatula until well incorporated.

2 Store in the refrigerator in an airtight container for up to 2 weeks. Bring to room temperature before use.

Pork Ramen

豚ラーメン

Kalua Pork and Cabbage Ramen

LEVEL 1

Serves 6

Prep time: 5 hours,
plus time to make
Ramen Soup Base
and Ramen Noodles
(optional)

I was inspired with this recipe by my Auntie Claudie Naauao, who lives in Hawaii. She suggested that I make a kalua pork version of ramen. I love the smoky flavor of kalua pork and how its tender pieces easily shred into delicate strings that soak up the soup base. I would suggest that you use a slow cooker for this to make it easier. The braised cabbage and sweet sautéed apples make it a complete dish and the liquid smoke gives it an instant smoky flavor.

To Make in Advance

Miso Base (page 3) or your base of choice

Ramen Noodles (page 13)

2 tbsp Hawaiian sea salt

1½ lbs (670 g) pork shoulder

2 tbsp rendered bacon fat (any fat or oil can be substituted)

2 tsp liquid smoke

1 head cabbage, quartered (I prefer Napa cabbage)

1 tbsp unsalted butter

2 apples, peeled and diced

1 tsp smoked paprika

Additional Toppings

6 green onions, chopped (1 tbsp per serving)

1 Sprinkle 1 tablespoon sea salt on each side of pork shoulder. In a slow cooker, add the bacon fat, set the pork shoulder on top, and pour the liquid smoke on top. Cover and cook for 3 hours on high. Add the cabbage and continue cooking until meat is tender and shreds easily, about 1 hour longer.

2 Transfer the pork to a cutting board and pull it into shreds with a fork. Transfer the cabbage to a bowl and discard the cooking juices; they will be too salty to use for anything.

3 In a medium frying pan over medium-high heat, melt the butter. Add the apples, sprinkle with paprika, and cook, stirring frequently until the apples are tender, about 10 minutes. Remove from the heat and season with salt and pepper.

4 Boil a pot of water for your noodles. In a separate saucepan, bring 2¼ cups (530 ml) Miso Base and 12 cups (2.8 L) chicken or vegetable stock to a boil, then lower heat and let simmer until it's ready to serve. Note: It's 3 tablespoons of base to every 1 cup (235 ml) stock. Use about 2 cups (475 ml) soup per serving. Right before serving, crank it back up to boil.

5 Boil the noodles—if fresh, boil for about 1 minute; if packaged, boil for about 2 minutes. As soon as they're done, drain well and separate into serving bowls.

6 Pour 2 cups (475 ml) soup over each bowl of noodles. Top each bowl with a small mound of shredded pork, cabbage, apple, and green onions.

Indonesian Pork Ramen with Coconut Curry Soup

LEVEL 1

Serves 6

Prep time: 30 minutes cooking time, 2 hours marinating, plus time to make Ramen Soup Base, Ramen Noodles (optional), Japanese Omelet (optional), and Fried String Potatoes (optional)

The recipe for the pork marinade in this recipe is from my friend Elisabeth who was given it by someone she met while hiking in Indonesia. I am forever grateful, as it's become a staple in my kitchen. This dish hits all the right notes—the aromatic flavors of the cumin, the sweetness of the bananas, the sliced tamagoyaki soaking up the coconut and curry broth, and the crunch of the fried string potatoes that stay crisp, even when drenched in soup. I usually marinate the pork and refrigerate it overnight to save time.

Juice of 1 lime

2 tbsp shoyu (soy sauce)

2 tbsp maple syrup or brown sugar

2 garlic cloves, minced

1 tbsp ground cumin

1 tbsp curry powder

½ tsp Sriracha or any chili paste

1 tbsp sesame oil

2 tbsp peanut butter

1½ lbs (670 g) pork tenderloin

1 tbsp unsalted butter

3 bananas, sliced on the diagonal

For the Soup

1½ cups (360 ml) coconut milk (¼ cup/60 ml per serving)

1 tbsp curry powder (½ teaspoon per serving)

Additional Toppings

1 bunch cilantro, leaves only (small pile per serving)

1 lime, cut into 6 segments (1 segment per serving)

1. Set a large ziplock bag in a bowl to keep it steady, then add the lime juice, shoyu, maple syrup or brown sugar, garlic, cumin, curry, Sriracha or other chili paste, sesame oil, and peanut butter. Put the pork loin in the bag, seal it, and move the marinade around so that the pork loins are well coated. Refrigerate and leave to marinate for at least 3 hours or up to 24 hours.

2. Prepare a gas or charcoal grill for medium-high heat. Cook the pork loin over direct heat for about 10 minutes per side, rotating until the internal temperature reaches 145°F (63°C). Transfer the meat to a cutting board and let it rest for at least 8 minutes—the meat should be pink inside.

3. Boil a pot of water for your noodles. In a separate saucepan, bring 2¼ cups (530 ml) Shio Base and 12 cups (2.8 L) chicken or vegetable stock to a boil. Whisk in the coconut milk and curry powder then reduce the heat and let simmer until ready to serve. Note: It's 3 tablespoons of base to every 1 cup (235 ml) chicken or vegetable stock. Use about 2 cups (475 ml) soup per serving. Right before serving, crank it back up to a boil.

4. In a small sauté pan over medium-high heat, cook the butter until it begins to brown. Add the bananas and cook until lightly browned and starting to crisp, about 1 minute on each side.

5. Boil the noodles—if fresh, boil for about 1 minute; if packaged, boil for about 2 minutes. As soon as they're done, drain well and separate into serving bowls.

6. Pour 2 cups (475 ml) soup over each bowl of noodles. Top each bowl with sliced pork, Japanese omelet, fried string potatoes, bananas, a little cilantro, and a segment of lime.

Tonkatsu Tonkotsu Ramen

LEVEL 3

Serves 6

Prep time: 1 hour, plus time to make Ramen Soup Base, Ramen Noodles (optional), Marinated Half-Cooked Egg (optional), and Menma (optional)

To Make in Advance

Tonkotsu Base (page 5)

Ramen Noodles (page 13)

Marinated Half-Cooked Egg (page 26)

Menma (page 20)

This porky ramen brings together two basic elements of the Japanese kitchen: *tonkatsu*, the breaded and fried cutlets that are so popular as a lunch dish and often included in bento boxes; and *tonkotsu*, the creamy white stock made from long-cooked pork bones, one of the classic bases for ramen.

1½ lbs (670 g) pork tenderloin, cut into ½-inch (1.25 cm) steaks
Salt and pepper, to season
½ cup (64 g) cornstarch (I prefer katakuriko, or Japanese potato starch)
2 eggs
1 tbsp water
2 cups (230 g) breadcrumbs (I prefer panko)
Vegetable oil, for frying

Additional Toppings

6 green onions, chopped (1 tbsp per serving)
Bean sprouts (small pile per serving)

1 Season both sides of the tenderloin steaks with salt and pepper.
2 Set up three dipping stations. Spread the cornstarch on a plate. Whisk the eggs and water in a medium-sized bowl. Pour the breadcrumbs on another plate.
3 In a deep-fry pan, add about ¾-inch (2 cm) oil. Heat on high to approximately 375°F/190°C or when a little panko sizzles immediately when added.
4 Dip seasoned pork in each station—cornstarch, then egg, then panko—covering both sides of each piece and shaking off any excess.
5 Set pork in frying pan to cook for about 2 minutes per side. Remove and set onto a paper towel until ready to use. Slice meat thinly on the diagonal.
6 Boil a pot of water for your noodles. In a separate saucepan, bring 12 cups (2.8 L) Tonkotsu Base to a boil, then lower the heat and let simmer until it's ready to serve. Use about 2 cups (475 ml) soup per serving. Right before serving, crank it back up to boil.

7 Boil the noodles—if fresh, boil for about 1 minute; if packaged, boil for about 2 minutes. As soon as they're done, drain well and separate into serving bowls.

8 Pour 2 cups (475 ml) soup over each bowl of noodles. Top each bowl with sliced pork, green onion, bean sprouts, marinated half-cooked egg, and menma.

Ohayogozaimasu (Good Morning Ramen)

LEVEL 1

Serves 6

Prep time: 30 minutes, plus time to make Ramen Soup Base, Ramen Noodles (optional), and Poached Eggs

To Make in Advance

Miso Base (page 3) or your base of choice

Ramen Noodles (page 13)

Poached Egg (page 21)

Ramen for breakfast, why not? I often make scrambled eggs cooked in brown butter with crisped sage leaves in the morning, so why would those ingredients be any less delicious in a bowl of noodles? I like to cook bacon in the oven. There's less mess to clean and the bacon ends up perfectly crisp. Just be sure to reserve the bacon fat; you'll need it for many of my basic recipes.

8 strips bacon (1½ strips per serving)
1 bunch sage leaves
¼ cup or ½ stick (55 g) unsalted butter

Additional toppings

1 bunch enoki mushrooms (small pile per serving)
1 avocado, sliced (3–4 slices per serving)
1 tomato, diced (small pile per serving)

1 Preheat oven to 400°F (200°C). Lay a piece of parchment paper on a baking sheet. Spread the bacon strips on the sheet and bake for about 20 minutes. Watch carefully as time will vary with ovens. They will crisp up with no need to turn the pieces over. Save your bacon grease in a jar because you can use it to make the ramen soup bases. Remove from the oven and set on a paper towel.

2 Roll the sage leaves into a cigar shape and cut perpendicular to the roll into long strips, or a chiffonade.

3 Heat the butter in a small skillet over high heat until the butter starts to brown. Immediately scatter the sage leaves in the pan and cook for about 10 seconds. Turn the heat off and use a slotted spoon to remove the sage to a paper towel. Keep the browned butter to drizzle over the ramen.

4 Boil a pot of water for your noodles. In a separate saucepan, bring 2¼ cups (530 ml) Miso Base and 12 cups (2.8 L) of broth to a boil, then lower the heat and let simmer until it's ready to serve. Note: It's 3 tablespoons of base to every 1 cup (235 ml) chicken or vegetable stock. Use about 2 cups (475 ml) soup per serving. Right before serving, crank it back up to boil.

5 Boil the noodles—if fresh, boil for about 1 minute; if packaged, boil for about 2 minutes. As soon as they're done, drain well and separate into serving bowls.

6 Pour 2 cups (475 ml) soup over each bowl of noodles. Top each bowl with, mushrooms, avocado slices, tomatoes, poached egg, a crumbled up half strip of bacon, and crispy sage; lay another whole piece of bacon on the side. Drizzle the browned butter over the top for added flavor.

Ranch-Style Ramen

LEVEL 2

Serves 6

Prep time: 1 hour, plus
time to make Ramen
Noodles (optional)
and Chashu (optional)

I learned to make this simple clear broth ramen from Sensei Rikisai at the Miyajima Ramen School in Osaka, Japan. It's relatively quick to make compared to more traditional styles of ramen and the ingredients are not hard to find, yet it still has a deep flavor. It's always a hit with my family. If you don't have access to kombu, you could substitute wakame, kelp granules, or a teaspoon of fish stock. The flavor will be slightly different but it will still be delicious!

To Make in Advance

Ramen Noodles
(page 13)

Chashu (page 22)

2 lbs (900 g) ground pork, not lean
½ lb (225 g) ground chicken
12 cups (2.8 L) water
4 pieces ginger (each 2 inches/5 cm long by ½ inch/ 6 mm wide), roughly cut on the diagonal, skin on
4 green onions (use the green part chopped large for soup and the white part for topping)
1 large rectangular piece kombu (about 10 inches/ 25 cm long), cut into large squares
1 large or 2 small dried shiitake mushrooms, crumbled
Salt, to taste

Additional Toppings
White parts of 4 green onions, thinly sliced, soaked in water for 5 minutes (1 tsp per serving)

1   In a large wok or stock pot, combine the ground pork and chicken with your hands. Add the water, a little at a time, squeezing the meat together and breaking up the fibers and fat until you get a sort of watery mush. You may want to wear disposable gloves to handle the raw meat.

2   Add the ginger, green onions, kombu, and shiitake mushrooms.

3   Turn heat to high. While the soup is coming to a boil, continue to stir with a large rubber spatula, picking up the mixture from the bottom and swiping the sides so that the meat does not stick. Stir frequently until the mixture comes to a boil and all of the meat has started to cook and the liquid is turning clear. This will take about 10 minutes. After the liquid turns clear, keep at a little bit above a simmer for another 30 minutes.

4   Drain the pork and chicken from the soup—once to get all of the larger pieces out with a thicker sieve and the second with a very fine sieve to get the remaining pieces out. For the second drain, return the soup to the wok and boil, then turn down to a simmer. Right before serving, crank it back up to a boil.

5 Prepare your chashu by frying quickly in a pan on both sides for 1–2 minutes to render the fat and make it crispy. Keep it ready to reheat right before placing on top of the ramen.

6 Pour 1½ cups (360 ml) soup into each serving bowl. Season individual bowls with salt, rather than the entire pot, to keep flavors consistent. Season until it's just a bit too salty because when added to the ramen, the noodles and extra water will take some of the salt taste away and balance it out.

7 Boil the noodles—if fresh, boil for about 1 minute; if packaged, boil for about 2 minutes. As soon as they're done, drain well and separate into the seasoned serving bowls.

8 Squeeze out the excess water from white parts of green onions and place a small mound on top. Also add the sliced chashu.

Chicken Ramen

チキンラーメン

Oven-Broiled Karaage Curry Ramen

LEVEL 2

Serves 6

Prep time: 1 hour, plus time to make Ramen Soup Base, Ramen Noodles (optional), Marinated Half-Cooked Egg (optional), and Garlic Chips (optional)

There are few foods I find more comforting than fried chicken—it ranks among my top five favorite foods in the world. *Karaage* is the Japanese version of fried chicken and I would eat it every day if I could. Since that just wouldn't be healthy, for this recipe, I cheat a bit and cook it in the oven. The chicken ends up wonderfully crisp and I don't have to deal with a pot of hot oil. The Golden Curry—a rich, thick, and instant curry that I add to the Miso Base—doesn't drench the karaage so it maintains its crunch. It's all the pleasure without the guilt.

To Make in Advance

Miso Base (page 3) or your base of choice

Ramen Noodles (page 13)

Marinated Half-Cooked Egg (page 26)

Garlic Chips (page 32)

1 cup (235 ml) shoyu (soy sauce)

1 cup (200 g) sugar

1 tsp minced garlic

1 tsp grated ginger

¼ cup (60 ml) mirin (sweet rice wine)

1 lb (455 g) chicken thighs

1 tbsp sesame oil

1 red onion, thinly sliced

¼ cup (32 g) cornstarch (I prefer katakuriko, or Japanese potato starch)

1 box of Golden Curry (Japanese instant curry that comes in a box)

Additional Toppings

1½ lemons, quartered (1 quarter slice per serving)

Roasted sesame seeds, for garnish

1 bunch arugula (I prefer Japanese mizuna lettuce; small pile per serving)

3 sheets nori (seaweed), quartered (2 squares per serving)

1. Add the shoyu, sugar, garlic, and ginger to a small saucepan and bring to boil. Once boiling, remove from the heat and add the mirin. Let cool to room temperature.
2. Rinse and pat dry the chicken thighs and cut each piece into bite-size pieces.
3. Add the chicken to a medium-sized bowl and cover with the marinade. Refrigerate and let marinate for at least 1 hour.
4. Heat the sesame oil in a medium-sized skillet on medium-high heat. Add the red onion and sauté until it starts to get charred around the edges. Set aside.
5. Set the oven rack at the top of the oven and preheat the broiler.
6. Drain the excess marinade from the bowl of chicken and sprinkle the chicken with cornstarch until all the pieces are liberally covered.
7. Place the chicken, so that no pieces are touching, on a parchment-lined baking sheet.
8. Broil for about 6 minutes, then flip and broil for an additional 5 minutes or until they are crispy and brown. Watch closely so they do not burn, as ovens will vary.
9. Set the chicken on a wire rack to cool.
10. Boil a pot of water for your noodles. In a separate saucepan, combine 2¼ cups (530 ml) Miso Base, 12 cups (2.8 L) of chicken or vegetable stock and 6 Golden Curry boullion squares to a boil, then lower the heat and let simmer until it's ready to serve. Note: It's 3 tablespoons base to every 1 cup (235 ml) chicken or vegetable stock. Use about 2 cups (475 ml) soup per serving. Right before serving, crank it back up to boil.
11. Boil the noodles—if fresh, boil for about 1 minute; if packaged, boil for about 2 minutes. As soon as they're done, drain well and separate into serving bowls.
12. Pour 2 cups (475 ml) soup over each bowl of noodles. Top with 3 pieces of chicken karaage, sautéed red onions, lettuce, marinated half-cooked egg, and garlic chips. Sprinkle with roasted sesame seeds and slip 2 nori squares into the broth. Right before serving, squeeze some lemon juice over the top.

Geng Gari Gai Ramen

LEVEL 2

Serves 6

Prep time:
45 minutes, plus time
to make Ramen Soup
Base and Ramen
Noodles (optional)

*To Make in
Advance*

Shio Base (page 10)

Ramen Noodles
(page 13)

In Thailand, I took a cooking class where I learned to make the most delicious Geng Gari Gai—a traditional dish from Southern Thailand with aromatic chicken and curry. Though I didn't have access to all the same ingredients that we had in Thailand, I was able to make a delicious soup using produce and seasonings found closer to home and combined it with my Shio Base.

1 tbsp peanut oil

1 tbsp minced garlic

½ cup (80 g) shallots, chopped

2 dried red chilies

2 cups (240 g) red bell pepper, seeded and chopped into bite-sized pieces

2 cups (300 g) Thai eggplant, chopped into bite-sized pieces

1½ cups (360 ml) coconut cream

1 tsp salt

¼ tsp white pepper

1 tsp ground turmeric

2 tsp ground coriander

1 tsp ground cumin

½ tsp ground cloves

1 tsp ginger, grated

1 tsp lemongrass paste

3 chicken thighs, skin removed, cut into bite-sized pieces

Salt and pepper, to season

2 tbsp fish sauce

2 limes, juice of ½ for squeezing over, the rest quartered for topping (I prefer Kaffir lime)

1 tbsp brown sugar

1½ cups (360 ml) chicken stock

Additional Toppings

1 bunch basil (I prefer Thai basil; a couple sprigs per serving)

1 Heat the peanut oil in a large skillet or wok over medium-high heat. Add the garlic and shallots and sweat for 2 minutes. Turn heat down to medium and add the chilies, red pepper, and eggplant. Continue to stir for 3–4 minutes until the eggplant starts to soften. Remove from the heat and transfer to a bowl.

2 In the same skillet or wok, heat the coconut cream, salt, pepper, turmeric, coriander, cumin, cloves, ginger, and lemongrass paste over low heat. Season the chicken, add it to the pan, and turn the heat to high. Then reduce the heat to a simmer, cover, and cook for about 15 minutes.

3 Add in the fish sauce, juice of ½ lime, brown sugar, and chicken stock. Simmer for an additional 10 minutes. Reserve 1 cup (235 ml) of curry sauce from the pan to use separately with your Shio Base.

4 Add the bowl of garlic, shallots, chilies, red pepper, and eggplant to the mixture and continue to simmer until ready to serve.

5 Boil a pot of water for your noodles. In a separate large pot, start preparing the stock for your Shio Base. To your 12 cups (2.8 L) chicken stock, whisk in 1½ cups (360 ml) Shio Base. Then whisk in the 1 cup (235 ml) curry sauce that you reserved from the pan. Heat this up to boil, then lower the heat and let simmer until ready to use. Right before serving, crank it back up to boil.

6 Boil the noodles—if fresh, boil for about 1 minute; if packaged, boil for about 2 minutes. As soon as they're done, drain well and separate into serving bowls.

7 Pour 2 cups (475 ml) soup over each bowl of noodles. Top with a generous helping of chicken, vegetables, and curry, and garnish with basil and a lime segment.

Chicken Meatball Ramen

LEVEL 2

Serves 6

Prep time:
40 minutes, plus
time to make Ramen
Soup Base, Ramen
Noodles (optional),
and Poached Egg
(optional)

My husband is Jewish so I've become pretty familiar with the light texture and fluffiness of a good matzah ball. I wanted to make a chicken meatball that's equally light and delicious so I borrowed the technique of adding club soda and whipped egg whites to the meat mixture. The Shio Base gives it the perfect balance of saltiness and the golden yolk of the poached egg mixes in to bring the "chicken and the egg" together again.

To Make in Advance

Shio Base (page 10) or
your base of choice

Ramen Noodles
(page 13)

Poached Egg (page 21)

2 egg whites

1 lb (455 g) ground chicken

2 tbsp carrot, finely grated

2 tbsp finely chopped wood ear mushrooms

4 shiso leaves, finely chopped

1 tbsp sugar

1 tbsp shoyu (soy sauce)

¼ cup (60 ml) seltzer or club soda

1 tsp onion powder

½ tsp garlic salt

¼ tsp pepper

¼ cup (30 g) panko breadcrumbs

Broth for Shio Base

12 cups (2.8 L) chicken or vegetable stock,
   fresh or store-bought

¾ cup or 1½ sticks (175 g) unsalted butter

¾ cup (175 ml) mirin (sweet rice wine)

1 large rectangular piece kombu (about
   10 inches/25 cm long), cut into large squares

12 dried shiitake mushrooms

Additional toppings

1 bunch daikon radish shoots (small pile per serving)

1 red pepper, seeded and julienned (¼ cup/35 g
   per serving)

1. Using a mixer or a whisk, whip the egg whites until soft peaks form.

2. In a medium-sized bowl, combine the chicken, carrot, mushrooms, mint, sugar, shoyu, seltzer, onion powder, garlic salt, and pepper until well combined.

3. Gently fold in the breadcrumbs and the egg whites until just combined. Let the mixture rest for 10 minutes.

4. In a large pot, start preparing the broth for your Shio Base. Combine the chicken or vegetable stock with butter, mirin, kombu, and mushrooms. Bring this to a low boil.

5. Make about 24 golf-ball-sized balls with the chicken mixture, enough for 2 per servings. The trick is to not overhandle the mixture, just gently scoop out and make them as quickly as possible, being careful not to squeeze at all when forming them. Wth a slotted spoon, drop them right into the stock you've prepared and cook in batches for about 6 minutes, uncovered.

6. Boil a pot of water for your noodles. Remove the chicken meatballs from your broth, take out the kombu and dried mushrooms and add your 2¼ cups (530 ml) Shio Base to the broth. It's 3 tablespoons of base for every 1 cup (235 ml) of stock. Heat this back up to a boil, then lower the heat and let simmer until ready to use. Right before serving, crank it back up to boil.

7. Boil the noodles—if fresh, boil for about 1 minute; if packaged, boil for about 2 minutes. As soon as they're done, drain well and separate into serving bowls.

8. Pour 2 cups (475 ml) soup over each bowl of noodles. Top each bowl with 4 meatballs, a small mound of daikon radish shoots, sweet red pepper, and a poached egg.

Ginger Chicken Ramen

LEVEL 1

Serves 6

**Prep time:
45 minutes, plus time
to make Ramen Soup
Base and Ramen
Noodles (optional)**

*To Make in
Advance*

....

Shoyu Base (page 8) or
your base of choice

....

Ramen Noodles
(page 13)

....

It's definitely not for everyone, but when ginger shines as the star flavor of a dish, I'm a fan. You can increase or reduce the amount as you please but you know where I stand. The crispy green beans, just-cooked shoyu egg scramble, and shredded carrots balance the intensity of the ginger, especially when mixed into the soup. It's always easiest to freeze your ginger before grating.

**2 boneless, skinless chicken breasts, thinly sliced on
the diagonal**

Salt and pepper, to season

3 tbsp grated ginger

3 tbsp sake

18 green beans, washed with tips cut (3 per serving)

**⅓ cup (45 g) cornstarch (I prefer katakuriko,
or Japanese potato starch)**

3 eggs

1½ tsp shoyu (soy sauce)

1 tsp sugar

1 tbsp unsalted butter

Additional Toppings

**2 medium-sized carrots, shredded (2 tbsp
per serving)**

Roasted sesame seeds, for garnish

1   Place the sliced chicken into the bottom of a deep medium-sized skillet.
2   Sprinkle the salt, pepper, ginger, and sake over the chicken. Cover with a drop lid or aluminum foil with a small hole in the center.
3   Bring to a boil, then lower to a simmer and cook about 8 minutes, or until liquid starts to evaporate.
4   Remove the chicken and set in a bowl. Let it cool and finely shred it. Keep the shredded chicken in the juices from the bowl until ready to serve.
5   In the same skillet used above, heat ¼-inch (6 mm) vegetable oil on medium-high.
6   In a shallow dish, dredge the green beans in the cornstarch until well coated.
7   Fry the green beans in batches in the oil on both sides until golden brown. Remove and set on a paper towel.

8   Boil a pot of water for your noodles. In a separate saucepan, bring 12 cups (2.8 L) Shoyu Base to a boil, then lower the heat and let simmer until it's ready to serve. Right before serving, crank it back up to boil.

9   Right before you are about to pour the soup in your bowls, you'll need to make your shoyu egg scramble. In a small bowl, combine the eggs, shoyu, and sugar. Beat well.

10 Heat 1 tablespoon butter in a medium skillet over high heat. When the butter starts to brown, pour in your beaten eggs and very quickly mix around with chopsticks.

11 When the eggs are barely cooked, remove from the pan and set in a bowl—they should be somewhat runny.

12 Boil the noodles—if fresh, boil for about 1 minute; if packaged, boil for about 2 minutes. As soon as they're done, drain well and separate into serving bowls.

13 Pour 2 cups (475 ml) soup over each bowl of noodles. Top each bowl with a large mound of shredded ginger chicken, shredded carrots, shoyu egg scramble, and roasted sesame seeds.

Beef Ramen

ビーフラーメン

Teriyaki Beef-Wrapped Asparagus Ramen

LEVEL 2

Serves 6

Prep time:
30 minutes, plus
time to make Ramen
Soup Base, Ramen
Noodles (optional),
Fried String
Potatoes (optional),
and Marinated
Half-Cooked Egg
(optional)

*To Make in
Advance*

....
Miso Base (page 3) or
your base of choice
....
Ramen Noodles
(page 13)
....
Fried String Potatoes
(page 34)
....
Marinated Half-
Cooked Egg (page 26)
....

When I was a kid, my mom made beef-wrapped asparagus appetizers whenever she hosted fancy parties. I felt so grown-up eating them and I loved how perfectly bite-sized they were. Now, I think they're the perfect addition to elevate any ramen. I found some sweet Momotaro tomatoes at a farmers' market in Santa Barbara and added them in for a pretty pop of color. You can add any fresh vegetables that you feel would complement it as well.

½ lb (225 g) thinly sliced beef sirloin (I prefer
   shabu shabu beef)
½ lb (225 g) asparagus spears, trimmed
4 tbsp shoyu (soy sauce)
4 tbsp sugar
1 tbsp grated ginger
½ tsp minced garlic
2 tsp sesame oil
½ lb (225 g) baby bok choy, rinsed and dried
   (you can substitute Swiss chard)
Sea salt, to season

Additional Toppings

1½ small tomatoes, sliced into eighths (I prefer
   Momotaro tomatoes; 2 slices per serving)
3 sheets nori, quartered (2 squares per serving)
Roasted sesame seeds, for garnish

1   Cut the raw beef slices in half and roll each asparagus spear in ½ slice of beef, pressing the meat around asparagus so that it is tightly rolled and stays secure.
2   In a small bowl, combine the shoyu, sugar, ginger, and garlic. Whisk to combine.
3   Heat 1 teaspoon sesame oil in a large skillet over medium-high heat. Add the rolled beef and asparagus and cook for about 5 minutes, turning throughout until all sides are lightly browned.

4   Pour the sauce mixture over the beef and asparagus and turn to coat. Remove and set onto a plate, then pour the remaining sauce over the top. When cool, slice each spear in half diagonally.

5   In the same skillet you used to brown the beef and asparagus, heat 1 teaspoon of sesame oil over high heat. Add the bok choy and quickly cook on both sides until tender, about 2 minutes. Remove and season with a sprinkle of sea salt.

6   Boil a pot of water for your noodles. In a separate saucepan, bring 2¼ (530 ml) cups Miso Base and 12 cups (2.8 L) broth to a boil, then lower the heat and let simmer until it's ready to serve. Note: It's 3 tablespoons of base to every 1 cup (235 ml) chicken or vegetable broth. Use about 2 cups (475 ml) soup per serving. Right before serving, crank it back up to a boil.

7   Boil the noodles—if fresh, boil for about 1 minute; if packaged, boil for about 2 minutes. As soon as they're done, drain well and separate into serving bowls.

8   Pour 2 cups (475 ml) soup over each bowl of noodles. Top each bowl with 4 halved slices of beef-wrapped asparagus, a small bunch of bok choy, 2 tomato slices, a pile of fried string potatoes, and a marinated half-cooked egg. Tuck 2 squares of nori into the soup, then sprinkle some roasted sesame seeds over for garnish.

Kobe Beef Tsukemen

LEVEL 1

Serves 4

**Prep time:
45 minutes, plus time
to make Ramen Soup
Base, Ramen Noodles
(optional), and
Roasted Garlic
Butter (optional)**

Kobe beef, the delicious and tender well-marbled beef from Kobe, a city in Japan's Hyogo prefecture, isn't exactly something you find at your grocery store every day, but when you do stumble across it, treat yourself to something divine. The real highlight of this dish is the style of this ramen. It's prepared as a *tsukemen*, where you drench your separated noodles into a flavor-rich warm soup. Look out for the pieces of kobe that come with a little square of beef suet, or beef fat. You can melt the suet and sear the meat in it for additional flavor and umami.

To Make in Advance

Shoyu Base (page 8) or
your base of choice

Ramen Noodles
(page 13)

Roasted Garlic Butter
(page 31)

1 tbsp lemon juice (I prefer Meyer lemons)

1 tbsp shoyu (soy sauce)

1 tbsp sake

1 tbsp mirin (sweet rice wine)

2 Kobe beef steaks or any well-marbled beef

Salt and pepper, to season

1 tbsp beef suet (beef fat that you can ask your butcher for)

⅓ cup (43 g) grated fresh horseradish

Additional Toppings

4 raw quail eggs

¼ cup (30 g) grated daikon (small mound per serving)

4 shiso leaves (1 leaf per serving)

1 lemon (1 thin slice per serving)

1. In a small bowl, whisk the lemon juice, shoyu, sake, and mirin to make a marinade.
2. Sprinkle the steak with salt and pepper.
3. Melt the suet in a medium-sized skillet over high heat. Add the steak and quickly sear on both sides, until just cooked, leaving the meat rare in the center.
4. Add the marinade to coat and remove the steak from the pan to rest, leaving the juices in the pan.
5. Reduce the marinade and pan juices for about 1 minute in the skillet.
6. Boil a pot of water for your noodles. In a separate saucepan, bring 4 cups (946 ml) Shoyu Base to a boil. Add the remaining cooking marinade and pan juices from the steak and whisk in the horseradish, then lower the heat and let simmer until it's ready to serve. Use 1 cup (235 ml) soup per serving. Right before serving, crank it back up to boil.
7. Cut the steak into small squares—the meat should be on the rare to medium-rare side.
8. Boil the noodles—if fresh, boil for about 1 minute; if packaged, boil for about 2 minutes. As soon as they're done, drain well and separate into serving bowls.
9. Add ½ of one cubed steak to the serving bowls. Top with a quail egg, mound of daikon, a shiso leaf, a thin slice of lemon, and a dollop of roasted garlic butter. Serve the soup in a separate bowl for dipping.

Sukiyaki Ramen

LEVEL 1

Serves 4

**Prep time:
30 minutes, plus time
to make Ramen Soup
Base, Ramen Noodles
(optional), Fried
Onions (optional),
and Black Garlic
Oil (optional)**

*To Make in
Advance*

Miso Base (page 3)
or your base of choice

Ramen Noodles
(page 13)

Fried Onions (page 33)

Black Garlic Oil
(page 30)

I love everything about *sukiyaki*—traditionally wafer-thin beef, served hot pot style by simmering with vegetables, tofu, and a jelly-type noodle, and often dipped in raw egg. Here, I've added quail eggs as a topping, in case you find a raw egg is too much. It cooks really quick so just make sure you have all of your other components ready to go.

½ cup (120 ml) shoyu (soy sauce)

½ cup (100 g) sugar

¼ cup (60 ml) mirin (sweet rice wine)

2 tbsp sake

1 tsp garlic

1 tsp ginger

1 medium-sized carrot, cut into matchsticks

¼ cup (30 g) daikon radish, cut into matchsticks

½ cup (75 g) red pepper, seeded and julienned

½ cup (35 g) cabbage, shredded (I prefer Napa cabbage)

4 mushrooms, thinly sliced (I prefer shiitake mushrooms)

1 block tofu, medium firmness, cut into bite-sized cubes

1 lb (455 g) sukiyaki beef or paper-thin slices of beef

Salt and pepper, to season

Additional toppings

4 green onions (1 tbsp per serving), chopped on the diagonal

8 raw quail eggs (optional)

1 Make the cooking liquid by whisking the shoyu, sugar, mirin, sake, garlic, and ginger together until combined.

2 Warm the liquid in a medium-sized skillet over a high heat. When it reaches a boil, turn down to medium-high heat and add the carrot, daikon radish, red pepper, cabbage, and mushrooms. Cook for 5 minutes, then remove with a slotted spoon and set aside.

3 Next cook the tofu for an additional 5 minutes. Remove it and set aside.

4   Season the beef, then add it and cook it very quickly. Leave it as rare as possible; the heat of the ramen soup will continue to cook it so it's ok if it's redder than is usually safe. Remove it and set aside.

5   Boil a pot of water for your noodles. In a separate saucepan, bring 1½ cups (360 ml) Miso Base and 8 cups (1.8 L) broth to a boil. Add the remaining cooking liquid from the sukiyaki to your soup base, then lower the heat and let simmer until it's ready to serve. Note: It's 3 tablespoons of base to every 1 cup (235 ml) chicken or vegetable broth. Use 2 cups (475 g) soup per serving. Right before serving, crank it back up to boil.

6   Boil the noodles—if fresh, boil for about 1 minute; if packaged, boil for about 2 minutes. As soon as they're done, drain well and separate into serving bowls.

7   Pour 2 cups (475 ml) soup over each bowl of noodles. Top each bowl with 3–4 pieces of sukiyaki meat, a pile of vegetables, a pile of tofu, green onions, 2 quail eggs, and fried onions, and drizzle black garlic oil over the soup.

Seafood Ramen

シーフードラーメン

Malaysian Curry Laksa Ramen

LEVEL 3

Serves 4

Prep time: 1 hour, plus time to make Ramen Soup Base and Ramen Noodles (optional)

To Make in Advance

....
Shio Base (page 10) or your base of choice
....
Ramen Noodles (page 13)
....

This recipe was created by my friend Emily Lai. This is a staple of Malaysian cuisine and stems from the basic ingredients of fresh roots and coconut milk. It shouldn't be too difficult to find dried shrimp, just look for fresh ones that are bright pink, coral-colored, and whole, as opposed to brown and falling apart.

1½-inch (4 cm) piece turmeric or 1 tbsp turmeric powder

1½-inch (4 cm) knob ginger, chopped (I prefer galangal)

3 medium-sized shallots, chopped

8 garlic cloves, chopped

15 dried chilies, seeds removed and soaked in hot water for 20 minutes

5 red chilies, chopped

4 cashews (I prefer candlenuts)

1½ oz (40 g) dried shrimp

1 tbsp ground coriander

1 lemongrass, white part only, chopped

1½ quarts (1.7 L) water

Pinch of salt, plus more to taste

1 chicken breast

1 lb (455 g) shrimp, peeled and halved lengthwise, with shells reserved (if shrimp have heads, also reserve)

4 tbsp vegetable oil

1 13.5-oz (400 ml) can coconut milk

¼ lb (115 g) mung bean sprouts (you can substitute sunflower or soybean sprouts)

Additional Toppings

2 hard-boiled eggs, peeled and halved (½ egg per serving)

¼ lb (115 g) green beans, cut into bite-sized pieces and blanched (1 oz/28 g per serving)

1 red chili, sliced (I prefer Fresno chillies; 1 tsp per serving)

1 handful mint, leaves removed (I prefer Vietnamese mint; small bunch per serving)

1 lime, quartered (1 wedge per serving)

1 Prepare the laksa paste by blending the turmeric, ginger, shallots, garlic, dried chilies, red chilies, cashews, dried shrimp, coriander, and lemongrass together in a food processor or blender until it turns into a paste.

2 In a medium pot with a lid, bring the water and a pinch of salt to a boil. Add the chicken breast, and when the water returns to a boil, cover and let the chicken steep in the hot water for 20 minutes. Do not open the lid.

3 Remove the chicken then return the water to a boil and add the shrimp. Cook for 5 minutes, then remove and let cool.

4 Add reserved shrimp shells and heads to the cooking liquid. Let simmer for 10 minutes, then strain out all solids.

5 Add 3/4 cup (175 ml) Shio Base and simmer for another 10 minutes.

6 Boil a large pot of water for your noodles.

7 Heat the oil in a large skillet over medium-high heat. Add the laksa paste and sauté until the oil starts to separate. Reserve a few tablespoons for your topping.

8 Add the coconut milk to your Shio soup infused with chicken and shrimp and bring it to a boil. Check for seasoning to see if more salt needs to be added.

9 Blanch the mung bean sprouts in the same ramen noodle water for 30 seconds and set aside.

10 Boil the noodles—if fresh, boil for about 1 minute; if packaged, boil for about 2 minutes. As soon as they're done, drain well and separate into serving bowls.

11 Pour 2 cups (475 ml) soup over each bowl of noodles. Top with blanched bean sprouts, hard-boiled egg, green beans, chili, mint, and a spoonful of the reserved laksa paste. Garnish with a lime wedge. If desired, top with chicken and shrimp meat.

Southern Crawfish Ramen

LEVEL 3

Serves 4

Prep time: 1 hour, plus time to make Ramen Soup Base and Ramen Noodles (optional)

Another great recipe that Emily Lai and I developed together! Although born in Malaysia, Emily now lives in San Francisco, where she operates The Rib Whip, a Southern BBQ truck, and a Malaysian pop-up called Masak | Masak. We had so much fun experimenting with different combinations for this Louisiana-style ramen. I was pleasantly surprised to be able to find all of the ingredients in my local grocery stores.

To Make in Advance

Shoyu Base (page 8) or your base of choice

Ramen Noodles (page 13)

2 lbs (900 g) cooked crawfish with shells
 (langostinos or shell-on shrimp can be substituted)

2½ quarts (2.8 L) water

½ cup (150 g) salt

1 tsp ground black pepper

1 tsp ground coriander

1 tsp ground cloves

2 tsp cayenne

2 tsp paprika

1 tsp oregano

1 tsp thyme

1 whole lemon, halved

1 whole sweet onion, peeled and sliced

4 whole garlic cloves, smashed

2 tbsp vegetable oil, divided

1 small onion, chopped

1 red bell pepper, seeded and chopped

2 celery stalks, chopped

6 oz (170 g) smoked sausage, sliced ¼ inch
 (6 mm) thick (I prefer andouille)

Additional Toppings

4 green onions, cut on the bias (1 tbsp per serving)
 (I prefer ramps)

Zest of 4 lemons (1 tsp per serving)

1 tsp gumbo file powder, optional (¼ tsp per serving)

1 De-shell the crawfish, saving the shells for step 2 and setting the meat aside for topping the soup.

2 Fill a large pot with the water and add the crawfish shells, salt, black pepper, coriander, cloves, cayenne, paprika, oregano, thyme, lemon (squeeze in juice and add halves), onion, and garlic. Bring to a boil over high heat for about 30 minutes. Save the stock for later use.

3 Heat 1 tablespoon oil in a large saucepan over medium-high heat. Add the onion, bell pepper, and celery (or what is called the "holy trinity") and let sweat for 10 minutes. Place in a bowl and set aside.

4 In the same saucepan used above, heat 1 tablespoon vegetable oil over medium-high heat. Add the sliced sausage and cook through, turning throughout, for about 5 minutes until browned.

5 Boil a pot of water for your noodles. In a separate large saucepan, combine 5 cups (1.2 L) Shoyu Base to 3 cups (700 ml) crawfish shell stock to 1½ cups (360 ml) holy trinity (step 3) and bring to a boil, then lower the heat and let simmer until you are ready to serve. Right before serving, crank it back up to a boil.

6 De-shell the crawfish when they are cooled and set aside.

7 Boil the noodles—if fresh, boil for about 1 minute; if packaged, boil for about 2 minutes. As soon as they're done, drain well and separate into serving bowls.

8 Pour 2 cups (475 ml) soup over each bowl of noodles. Top each bowl with a small pile of crawfish, holy trinity, sausage, green onions, lemon zest, and a sprinkle of file powder. Garnish with a crawfish head.

Egg Drop Ramen

LEVEL 3

Serves 4

Prep time:
30 minutes, plus time
to make Ramen Soup
Base and Ramen
Noodles (optional)

To Make in
Advance

....

Shio Base (page 10)
or your base of choice

....

Ramen Noodles
(page 13)

....

This is another recipe that I developed with help from my friend Emily Lai. Emily was born in Kuala Lumpur, Malaysia, and raised in the restaurant business. She generously shared her method for making traditional egg drop soup as the base for this ramen. She published the original in *Vogue* magazine, so this is something special.

8 cups (1.8 L) chicken stock

1 ham hock or substitute ½ lb (225 g)
    smoked sausage or bacon

1½ cups or ¼ lb (115 g) Napa cabbage,
    roughly chopped

Salt, to season

1 lb (455 g) sea bass, skin removed, cut into
    4 portions

1 tsp sesame oil

¼ lb (115 g) snap peas

4 eggs

4 tsp Shaoxing wine (you can substitute sake
    or dry sherry)

Additional Toppings

1½ cups or ¼ lb (115 g) Napa cabbage, julienned
    (1 oz/28 g per serving)

2 oz (55 g) wood ear mushrooms (½ oz/15 g
    per serving)

Zest of 4 lemons (1 tsp per serving)

1   In a large pot, bring the chicken stock, 1½ cups (360 ml) Shio Base, ham hock, and cabbage to a boil. Simmer for 1 hour so that the soup can absorb the flavors of the ham hock and cabbage.

2   Lightly salt both sides of the sea bass and immerse in the soup. Cook for 5–7 minutes to poach. Remove the fish and set aside.

3   Strain the ham hock and the cabbage out of the soup and discard. Bring the liquid to a boil, then lower the heat and let simmer until you are ready to serve.

4   Heat the sesame oil in medium skillet and sauté the snap peas for about 2 minutes. Sprinkle with salt and remove from the heat.

5   In a small bowl, whisk the eggs and Shaoxing wine together.

6   Boil the noodles—if fresh, boil for about 1 minute; if packaged, boil for about 2 minutes. As soon as they're done, drain well and separate into serving bowls.

7   Crank the heat up on the soup base to boil, turn off the heat and immediately whisk in the egg mixture with a chopstick. You'll see the eggs cook and create light strings throughout the soup.

8   Pour 2 cups (475 ml) soup over each bowl of noodles. Top each bowl with a portion of sea bass, sautéed snap peas, a pile of julienned cabbage, mushrooms, and lemon zest.

Crispy Soft Shell Crab Ramen

LEVEL 2

Serves 6

Prep time: 1 hour, plus time to make Ramen Soup Base, Ramen Noodles (optional), Marinated Half-Cooked Egg (optional), and Roasted Garlic Butter (optional)

To Make in Advance

Shoyu Base (page 8) or your base of choice

Ramen Noodles (page 13)

Marinated Half-Cooked Egg (page 26)

Roasted Garlic Butter (page 31)

One of my all-time favorite foods is fried soft-shell crab with its crispy delicate legs and the fact that you can eat the entire body, bite after juicy bite. They are way less work than a hard-shell crab and, in my opinion, even tastier. Most Asian food markets carry them frozen, so there should be no problems finding them in the off-season. I like to cook these under the broiler, and have found that as long as you remove and press out any excess water from the crabs before dredging them with *katakuriko* or cornstarch, they cook up perfectly golden.

6 whole soft-shell crabs
¼ cup (32 g) cornstarch (I prefer katakuriko, or Japanese potato starch)
Nonstick cooking spray

Additional Toppings

12 squares nori (2 squares per serving)
¼ lb (340 g) fresh spinach (2 oz/55 g per serving)
1 avocado, sliced (3–4 slices per serving)
1 bunch enoki mushrooms (small pile per serving)
1 cup (235 ml) yuzu citrus juice (you can substitute lime juice; 2 tbsp per serving)

1 Set the oven rack to 4–6 inches (10–15 cm) from the heating element and preheat the broiler.
2 Gently squeeze out any water from the soft-shell crabs and dab lightly with a paper towel. Lightly dredge the soft-shell crabs on both sides with cornstarch and place on a lined cookie sheet.
3 Spray the crabs with nonstick cooking spray on both sides. Broil for about 5 minutes, then flip and broil for an additional 5 minutes or until they are crispy and brown. Watch closely so they do not burn, as ovens will vary.
4 Boil a pot of water for your noodles. In a separate saucepan, bring 12 cups (2.8 L) Shoyu Base to a boil, then lower the heat and let simmer until it's ready to serve. Right before serving, crank it back up to a boil.

5 Boil the noodles—if fresh, boil for about 1 minute; if packaged, boil for about 2 minutes. As soon as they're done, drain well and separate into serving bowls.

6 Pour 2 cups (475 ml) soup over each bowl of noodles. Slip 2 nori squares into the broth. Top with soft-shell crab, spinach, avocado slices, mushrooms, 2 tablespoons lime juice, marinated half-cooked egg, and a scoop of roasted garlic butter.

Furikake Salmon Ramen

LEVEL 1

Serves 6

Prep time:
30 minutes, plus
time to make Ramen
Soup Base, Ramen
Noodles (optional),
and Half-Cooked Egg
(optional)

To Make in Advance

....

Shoyu Base (page 8) or
your base of choice

....

Ramen Noodles
(page 13)

....

Marinated Half-
Cooked Egg (page 26)

....

This recipe is great because if you don't have the ramen soup base or fresh ramen noodles ready, you can eat the salmon on its own with some rice and a vegetable. I happen to love the salmon on ramen because the *furikake* condiment adds an additional crunchy texture and flavor.

24 oz (680 g) salmon fillet, skin on (ask for thickest part)

¼ cup (60 g) mayonnaise (I prefer Japanese mayonnaise that you can find at Japanese grocers)

1 tbsp shoyu (soy sauce)

1 tsp sesame oil (I prefer the Kadoya brand because it is very strong)

¼ cup (26g) furikake (Japanese condiment made from sesame seeds, seaweed, and salt)

Additional Toppings

1½ cups (105 g) mushrooms, julienned (I prefer shiitake; ¼ cup/17 g per serving)

¾ cup (40 g) chives, chopped (2 tbsp per serving)

1½ lemons, quartered (1 quarter per serving)

1   Set the oven to broil. Place the salmon, skin side down, on a baking sheet lined with foil or a non-stick liner. In a small bowl, whisk together the mayonnaise, shoyu, and sesame oil.

2   Using a spatula, evenly spread the mixture in a thin layer over the salmon.

3   Evenly sprinkle furikake over the salmon to lightly coat it.

4   Broil the salmon for about 8 minutes, or until just done; this varies depending on the thickness of the fillet (do not overcook).

5   Remove from the broiler and slice into 4 even portions, about 1½ inches (4 cm) wide. Remove the salmon skin.

6   Boil a pot of water for your noodles. In a separate saucepan, bring 12 cups (2.8 L) Shoyu Base to a boil, then lower the heat and let simmer until it's ready to serve. Right before serving, crank it back up to boil.

7 Boil the noodles—if fresh, boil for about 1 minute; if packaged, boil for about 2 minutes. As soon as they're done, drain well and separate into serving bowls.

8 Pour 2 cups (475 ml) soup over each bowl of noodles. Top with furikake salmon, mushrooms, chives, and a marinated half-cooked egg. Squeeze the lemon on right before eating, and enjoy while it's piping hot!

Sweet Chili Salmon Ramen

LEVEL 2

Serves 6

**Prep time:
20 minutes, plus time
to make Ramen Soup
Base, Ramen Noodles
(optional), and
Roasted Garlic
Butter (optional)**

*To Make in
Advance*

Shoyu Base (page 8) or
your base of choice

Ramen Noodles
(page 13)

Roasted Garlic Butter
(page 31)

The salmon on its own is one of my mom's favorite dishes, which I make for her every time she visits. I thought it would be great on ramen because the extra-crispy salmon skin gives it texture and it goes well with broccoli and broccolini. The tenderness of a freshly made menma or seasoned and simmered bamboo shoots, perfectly steamed broccoli drizzled with sesame oil and a swirl of roasted garlic butter make this one of my favorites, too.

6 oz (170 g) salmon fillet, skin on (1 oz/28 g
   per serving)
Salt and pepper, to season
2 tsp vegetable oil, divided
1 bunch broccoli, diced (you can substitute
   broccolini)
4 tbsp shoyu (soy sauce)
2 tbsp sweet chili sauce
1 tbsp sesame oil

1   Lightly season both sides of the salmon fillet.
2   Heat 1 teaspoon of vegetable oil in a medium-sized skillet over medium-high heat. Add the broccoli, sprinkle with salt and pepper and sauté for about 1 minute per side, then add 3 tablespoons of water and cover to let steam for an additional 2 minutes. Remove and set aside.
3   To the same pan, heat 1 teaspoon of vegetable oil in a medium-sized skillet over medium-high heat. Add the salmon, skin-side down and cover to steam for about 6 minutes or until the salmon flesh just turns opaque.
4   Remove the salmon and face skin side up on a cutting board. Gently remove the skin by running a knife along the underside of the skin and the salmon and return the skin to the pan. Fry it over high heat on both sides for about 2 minutes until it gets crispy. Remove and set on a paper towel.
5   To the same pan, add the shoyu, sweet chili sauce, and sesame oil and combine over medium heat until sauce bubbles.

6   Right before serving, return the salmon fillets to the pan and turn them in the sauce until completely covered.

7   Boil a pot of water for your noodles. In a separate saucepan, bring 12 cups (2.8 L) of Shoyu Base to a boil. then lower the heat and let simmer until you are ready to serve. Use about 2 cups (475 ml) soup per serving. Right before serving, crank it back up to a boil.

8   Cut the fried salmon skin into small strips and set aside.

9   Boil the noodles—if fresh, boil for about 1 minute; if packaged, boil for about 2 minutes. As soon as they're done, drain well and separate into serving bowls.

10 Pour 2 cups (475 ml) of piping hot soup in each warmed bowl. Top each bowl with a fillet of cooked salmon, a couple of branches of broccoli, a small mound of menma, and a dollop of garlic butter. Finally, sprinkle the fried salmon-skin strips on top.

California Ramen

LEVEL 2

Serves 6

Prep time:
20 minutes, plus
time to make Ramen
Soup Base, Ramen
Noodles (optional),
and Marinated Half-
Cooked Egg

Being a California native, I love the fresh, accessible ingredients found in a California roll. During crab season, our family always eats a ton of fresh Dungeness crabs and if you have access to any, this recipe is pretty simple to pull together. Most grocery stores carry cooked Alaskan king crab legs that you can take home and crack open—no fuss. I've recommended the Shoyu Base here as I think it best complements the seafood, but again, use whatever you have on hand or have decided to make. This recipe can be made in 20 minutes, but the speed of this is down to the additional toppings and the base, noodles, and eggs being prepped ahead of time.

To Make in Advance

Shoyu Base (page 8) or
your base of choice

Ramen Noodles
(page 13)

Marinated Half-
Cooked Egg (page 26)

2 lbs (900 g) cooked fresh crab (I prefer Dungeness)

1 tsp olive oil

¾ cup or 1½ sticks (170 g) unsalted butter

6 tsp minced garlic

½ lemon

Additional Toppings

1 cucumber, julienned (small bunch per serving)

1 avocado, sliced (couple slices per serving)

3 green onions, chopped (½ tbsp per serving)

1 lemon, cut into 6 segments (1 segment per serving)

2 sheets nori (seaweed), sliced into 6 pieces (2 pieces per serving)

Shichimi togarashi (Japanese mixed chili pepper spice), optional

1 Crack the crab and set aside.

2 Boil a pot of water for your noodles. In a separate saucepan, bring 12 cups (2.8 L) Shoyu Base to a boil, then lower the heat and let it simmer until it's ready to serve. Right before serving, crank it back up to a boil.

3 In a small saucepan, heat the olive oil and butter, then add the garlic and squeeze the lemon over it. Cook until just sizzling.

4 Boil the noodles—if fresh, boil for about 1 minute; if packaged, boil for about 2 minutes. As soon as they're done, drain well and separate into serving bowls.

5 Pour 2 cups (475 ml) soup over each bowl of noodles. Top with cracked crab, cucumber, avocado, green onion, and marinated half-cooked egg. Drizzle the garlic butter over the crab and sprinkle shichimi togarashi on the avocado. Tuck the nori into the soup. If you want to warm your crab, put a handful in a small sieve and heat it in the noodle water for 10 seconds before adding it in.

Spicy Ramen

スパイシーラーメン

Spicy Base

LEVEL 1

Serves 6

Prep time: 20 minutes

I most often use this spicy base with the Miso Base (page 3), but it can be used with any base to add a rich and spicy complexity that isn't mouth-numbing but definitely gives it a nice kick. Add more or less of it depending on how spicy you like your ramen.

16 small shishito peppers, whole (you can substitute 3 green bell peppers, seeded)

2 green chili peppers, seeded and quartered

2 tsp red pepper flakes

½ cup (120 ml) sesame oil

1 In a blender, combine the green bell peppers, green chili peppers, and red pepper flakes. Slowly add in the sesame oil to emulsify.

2 Add ½ cup (120 ml) of Spicy Base for each 2-cup (475-ml) serving to any Ramen Soup Base.

Chorizo Miso Ramen

LEVEL 2

Serves 6

Prep time: 45 minutes, plus time to make Ramen Soup Base, Ramen Noodles (optional), and Poached Egg (optional)

To Make in Advance

Miso Base (page 3) or your base of choice

Ramen Noodles (page 13)

Poached Egg (page 21)

The inspiration for this chorizo-infused miso base came to me when I was standing in line with my sister Kathleen at La Super Rica Taqueria, the Santa Barbara taco stand made famous by Juila Child. I was excited to discover how well the chorizo blended into the soup base. Then I added more spicy chorizo on top. The result is a vibrant, full-flavor Mexican take on ramen.

½ red onion, peeled

2 red peppers, seeded

2 green chilies, seeded

1 tbsp vegetable oil

3 ears sweet white corn (½ ear per serving)

1 lb (455 g) chorizo, casings removed

Additional Toppings

1 bunch kale (small pile per serving)

1 bunch radishes, sliced (3 slices per serving)

1   Add the onion, peppers, and chilies to a food processor and pulse until mixture is finely chopped.

2   Heat the oil in a large skillet over medium-high heat. Add the mixture and cook for 10 minutes. Remove from the heat and set aside in a bowl.

3   Steam the corn, let cool, then de-kernel it. Set aside.

4   In the same skillet you used for the mixture above, add the chorizo to the pan. As it cooks, break it into small pieces with a wooden spoon. Cook until it is browned and remove from heat.

5   Boil a pot of water for your noodles. In a separate saucepan, bring 2¼ cups (530 ml) Miso Base and 12 cups (2.8 L) broth to a boil. Add 6 tablespoons of cooked chorizo to your soup, then lower the heat and let simmer until you are ready to serve. Note: It's 3 tablespoons of base to every 1 cup (235 ml) chicken or vegetable stock. Use about 2 cups (475 ml) soup per serving. Right before serving, crank it back up to a boil.

6   Boil the noodles—if fresh, boil for about 1 minute; if packaged, boil for about 2 minutes. As soon as they're done, drain well and separate into serving bowls.

7   Pour 2 cups (475 ml) soup over each bowl of noodles. Top each bowl with a small mound of corn and chorizo; raw kale; about ¼ cup (40 g) of the onion, pepper, chili mixture; radishes; and a poached egg.

Mapo Tofu Ramen

LEVEL 3

Serves 4

Prep time: 1 hour, plus time to make Ramen Soup Base, Ramen Noodles (optional), and Poached Egg (optional)

To Make in Advance

Tonkotsu Base (page 5)

Ramen Noodles (page 13)

Poached Egg (page 21)

This is another great recipe that my friend Emily Lai helped me to develop. Emily is a seasoned restaurant owner who worked for chef Zak Pelaccio in New York, where she managed both Fatty Crab and opened 230Fifth with him. We are lucky to have her background and expertise in helping make this delicious rendition of Mapo Tofu Ramen full of spice and flavor. The Tonkotsu Base gives it the perfect thickness and the spice level is just right.

4 tbsp cornstarch

4 tbsp water

1 tbsp vegetable oil

2 garlic cloves, minced

1 shallot, minced

½ lb (225 g) ground pork

1 tsp salt

4 oz (115 g) shiitake mushrooms, sliced, divided

1 tbsp chili sauce (I prefer Sambal Oelek)

4 tbsp Shaoxing wine, divided (you can substitute dry sherry)

1 block medium firm tofu, cubed

1 tbsp sesame oil

1 tbsp chili oil

Additional Toppings

4 green onions, chopped (1 tbsp per serving)

1 bunch daikon radish sprouts (you can substitute alfalfa sprouts; small pile per serving)

1 tsp shichimi togarashi, optional (1 pinch per serving)

1 In a small bowl, whisk the cornstarch and water to make a slurry.
2 Heat the vegetable oil in a medium skillet, sweat the garlic and shallot over medium-high heat for approximately 30 seconds.
3 Add the pork and break it up into small pieces. Sprinkle with salt.
4 Add in half the shiitake mushrooms and continue to stir until pork is fully cooked.
5 Stir in the chili sauce.

6 Pour in half the dry sherry to deglaze the pan, stirring to pick up any bits from the bottom of the pan.

7 Heat 8 cups (1.8 L) of Tonkotsu Base in a large pot. Add the pork mixture and tofu and simmer for 10 minutes.

8 Heat the sesame oil in a medium-sized saucepan over medium-high heat. Add the remaining shiitake mushrooms, sprinkle with salt and sauté for 3–4 minutes. Deglaze with the rest of the dry sherry.

9 Crank up the heat for your Tonkotsu Base, add the chili oil and the cornstarch slurry to thicken. Keep at a boil until ready to serve.

10 Boil the noodles—if fresh, boil for about 1 minute; if packaged, boil for about 2 minutes. As soon as they're done, drain well and separate into serving bowls.

11 Pour 2 cups (475 ml) soup over each bowl of noodles. Top each bowl with green onion, daikon radish sprouts, sautéed shiitake mushrooms, and a poached egg, and sprinkle with shichimi togarashi for extra kick.

Spicy Tofu Ramen

LEVEL 2

Serves 6

Prep time:
20 minutes, plus
time to make
Ramen Soup Base,
Spicy Base, Ramen
Noodles (optional),
Agedashi-Doufu,
Menma (optional),
and Roasted Nori
(optional)

This recipe incorporates the Spicy Base with five other To Make in Advance recipes that can all be prepared ahead of time. I know it seems daunting to think about pulling this together, but the only recipe that really needs to be done the day you plan to eat it is the Agedashi-Doufu. Everything else can be done days before so that it takes just 30 minutes to get this to the table.

Additional Toppings

1 large package aburaage tofu (½ pocket per serving)
1 bunch mizuna lettuce (you can substitute arugula; small pile per serving)
12 raw quail eggs (optional)

To Make in Advance

Miso Base (page 3)
or your base of choice

Spicy Base (page 91)

Ramen Noodles
(page 13)

Agedashi-Doufu
(page 136)

Menma (page 20)

Roasted Nori (page 96)

1 If using, cut the roasted nori into small strips with kitchen scissors.
2 On an ungreased baking sheet, broil the aburaage tofu for about 2 minutes until it crisps up. Julienne into small strips.
3 Prepare the Agedashi-Doufu according to the recipe without the sauce accompaniment.
4 Boil a pot of water for your noodles. In a separate saucepan, combine 2¼ cups (530 ml) Miso Base, 12 cups (1.8 L) chicken or vegetable stock and 3 cups (700 ml) Spicy Base to a boil, then lower the heat and let simmer until it's ready to serve. Note: It's 3 tablespoons of base to every 1 cup (235 ml) chicken or vegetable stock. Use about 2 cups (475 ml) soup per serving. Right before serving, crank it back up to a boil.
5 Boil the noodles—if fresh, boil for about 1 minute; if packaged, boil for about 2 minutes. As soon as they're done, drain well an separate into serving bowls.
6 Pour 2 cups (475 ml) soup over each bowl of noodles. Top each bowl with a couple squares of Agedashi-Doufu, a pile of aburaage tofu strips, a small pile of arugula, a portion of menma, and 2 quail eggs. Finish with a sprinkling of roasted nori.

Spicy Pork Tantanmen

LEVEL 2

Serves 6

Prep time: 30 minutes, plus time to make Ramen Noodles (optional

To Make in Advance

....

Ramen Noodles (page 13)

....

On my ramen tour of Tokyo, I was taken to LaShowHan for *tantanmen*. The name translates to "red hot chili noodle," and the dish is a Japanese adaptation of a Szechuan-style spicy noodle dish known as Dan Dan noodles. I ordered a spectacular *mazemen* (brothless) style premium tantanmen with the perfect amount of heat—not too overpowering but with just enough kick to remind you of what it is. Without a heavy soup, the flavors of the individual spices stood out. The owner, Kenichi Okada, even took a selfie with our group. It's one of my favorite souvenirs from the trip. His tantanmen is the inspiration for this recipe, so I've tried to make my best Kenichisan, but if you want the real deal, you'll have to visit his shop in Tokyo (page 157).

1 red bell pepper

2 tbsp sesame oil

1 lb (455 g) ground pork

2 tsp chili oil

1 tsp salt

1 tbsp sugar

1 tbsp shoyu (soy sauce)

2 tbsp chili paste

¼ cup (60 g) sesame paste or tahini

⅛ tsp ground Szechuan peppercorns (you can substitute Tasmanian pepper)

3 cups (700 ml) chicken stock

Additional Toppings

6 green onions, chopped (1 tbsp per serving)

6 tbsp unsalted peanuts, crushed (1 tbsp per serving)

1 bunch daikon radish sprouts (you can substitute alfalfa sprouts; small pile per serving)

Sesame oil

3 tsp chili paste (½ tsp per serving)

1. Heat the whole pepper over an open flame on a gas stove or grill until all sides are completely black and charred.
2. Remove the skin from the pepper and slice open, removing the stem and seeds.
3. Purée the pepper in a food processor or a blender. Set aside.
4. Heat the sesame oil in a wok or large skillet over medium-high heat.
5. Add the ground pork and cook until no longer pink, breaking it up with a wooden spoon. Remove the pork and pulse in a food processor until it becomes a fine mince.
6. Warm the chili oil in the wok at medium-high heat and add the minced pork.
7. Stir in the salt, sugar, shoyu, chili paste, sesame paste, and ground peppercorns and fry until all of the aromatics combine.
8. Boil a pot of water for your noodles. Add in the chicken stock, bring to a boil and turn down to simmer for 10 minutes to absorb all of the spices. Stock should evaporate a little and the sauce will be thick.
9. Boil the noodles—if fresh, boil for about 1 minute; if packaged, boil for about 2 minutes. As soon as they're done, drain well and separate into serving bowls.
10. Pour ¾ cup (175 ml) of the sauce into a bowl, top with noodles and garnish with green onions, peanuts, daikon radish sprouts, a drizzle of sesame oil, and chili paste.

Vegetable Ramen

野菜ラーメン

Simmered Nasubi Ramen

LEVEL 2

Serves 4

**Prep time:
30 minutes, plus time
to make Ramen Soup
Base, Ramen Noodles
(optional), Japanese
Omelet (optional),
and Miso Butter
(optional)**

My mom always served *nasubi*, or Japanese eggplant, in the most appealing way, leaving the stem intact and slicing through the flesh so that it fanned out on the plate. I love this presentation of the eggplant and red cabbage on top of ramen, with its purple hues.

4 Japanese eggplants
Salt and pepper, to season
2 tbsp shoyu (soy sauce)
2 tbsp mirin (sweet rice wine)
1 tbsp rice wine vinegar
1 tsp sugar
1 tsp sesame oil

To Make in Advance

Tonkotsu Base (page 5)
or your base of choice
....

Ramen Noodles
(page 13)
....

Japanese Omelet
(page 18)
....

Miso Butter (page 35)
....

Additional Toppings

½ head red cabbage, shredded (small mound per serving)
2 tsp grated ginger (½ tsp per serving)
2 green onions, chopped (1 tsp per serving)

1 Cut the eggplant lengthwise in ¼-inch (6 mm) strips, leaving the stem on so that they can fan out. Lightly season both sides.
2 In a small bowl, combine the shoyu, mirin, rice wine vinegar, and sugar. Whisk to combine.
3 Heat the sesame oil in a large skillet over medium-high heat. Add the eggplant, fanning each one out so they are lying flat and none are touching. Cook for about 3 minutes on each side until they are lightly browned and the meat has softened. Repeat until all the eggplant is cooked.
4 Pour the sauce mixture over the eggplant and turn to evenly coat. Remove the eggplant and set onto a plate; pour the remaining sauce over the top.

5   Boil a pot of water for your noodles. In a separate saucepan, bring 8 cups (1.8 L) Tonkotsu Base to a boil, then lower the heat and let simmer until it's ready to serve. Use about 2 cups (475 ml) soup per serving. Right before serving, crank it back up to boil.

6   Boil the noodles—if fresh, boil for about 1 minute; if packaged, boil for about 2 minutes. As soon as they're done, drain well and separate into serving bowls.

7   Pour 2 cups (475 ml) soup over each bowl of noodles. Top each bowl with 1 fanned eggplant, a mound of red cabbage, grated ginger, green onion, Japanese omelet, and miso butter.

Kabocha Ramen

LEVEL 3

Serves 6

Prep time: 1 hour,
plus time to make
Ramen Soup Base,
Ramen Noodles
(optional), Marinated
Half-Cooked Egg
(optional), and
Roasted Garlic Butter
(optional)

To Make in Advance

Shoyu Base (page 8)

Ramen Noodles
(page 13)

Marinated Half-
Cooked Egg (page 26)

Roasted Garlic Butter
(page 31)

Kabocha ranks among my favorite winter Japanese squash. It has a rich and nutty flavor and because the skin is edible when cooked, there's no peeling required. In this ramen, the bitterness and spice of the mizuna lettuce balances the sweetness of the squash to deliver a nice balance. Since the kabocha is steeped in shoyu, the Shoyu Base goes perfectly and the fried shiso leaf gives it a surprise crunch to start your first bite.

½ medium-sized kabocha (Japanese squash)

2 tbsp shoyu (soy sauce)

1 tsp salt

½ tsp dashi granules

½ cup (100 g) sugar

¼ cup (60 ml) mirin (sweet rice wine)

1 cup (235 ml) water

Tempura Batter

1 egg

1 cup (235 ml) cold water

1¼ cups (155 g) all-purpose flour, sifted

Vegetable oil, for frying

6 shiso leaves

Additional Toppings

1 bunch buna shimeji mushrooms (small mound per serving)

1 bunch arugula (I prefer mizuna lettuce; small bunch per serving)

1   Cut the kabocha in half and remove the seeds with a spoon. Save one half for later. Cut the stem and bottom off of the remaining half and cut into 1½-inch (4 cm) cubes. No need to take the skin off.

2   In a medium skillet, whisk the shoyu, salt, dashi, sugar, mirin, and water. Bring to a boil and then reduce to simmer.

3   Add the kabocha in one layer so that each piece is touching the sauce. The sauce should almost cover the kabocha.

4   Simmer, uncovered, until the kabocha is soft, approximately 45 minutes. Turn each piece over halfway through cooking. When finished, the liquid should be almost gone.

5   Make a tempura batter out of the egg, cold water, and flour. Add ½-inch (6 mm) oil to a medium skillet on medium-high heat. Dip the shiso leave(s) into the batter mixture one at a time. When a little flour thrown in starts to sizzle, fry the shiso leaves, making sure they do not touch each other in the pan. Fry on both sides for about 10 seconds each, then set on a paper towel to remove excess oil until ready to use.

6   Boil a pot of water for your noodles. In a separate saucepan, bring 12 cups (1.8 L) Shoyu Base to a boil, then lower the heat and let simmer until you are ready to serve. Use about 2 cups (475 ml) soup per serving. Right before serving, crank it back up to a boil.

7   Boil the noodles—if fresh, boil for about 1 minute; if packaged, boil for about 2 minutes. As soon as they're done, drain well and separate into serving bowls.

8   Pour 2 cups (475 ml) soup over each bowl of noodles. Top each bowl with kabocha, a shisho leaf, mushrooms, arugula, a marinated half-cooked egg, and a tablespoon of roasted garlic butter.

Mushroom-Lovers' Ramen

LEVEL 2

Serves 4

Prep time: 1 hour, plus time to make Ramen Soup Base, Ramen Noodles (optional), and Marinated Half-Cooked Egg (optional)

To Make in Advance

....

Shio Base (page 10) or your base of choice
....
Ramen Noodles (page 13)
....
Marinated Half-Cooked Egg (page 26)
....

Hello fellow fungi lovers! With so many Japanese mushrooms to choose from, just go with whatever is fresh for the season. The only mushrooms I wouldn't recommend here are matsutake mushrooms because of their high cost and strong flavor. If you are lucky enough to get your hands on those, make a dish where they are the highlight; in this dish, any other mushroom varieties works, so pick four of your favorites.

¼ lb (115 g) forest nameko mushrooms, divided

¼ lb (115 g) buna shimeji mushrooms, divided

¼ lb (115 g) enoki mushrooms, divided

¼ lb (115 g) shiitake mushrooms, divided

8 cups or 2 qt (1.9 L) chicken or vegetable stock

1 cup (230 g) heavy whipping cream

4 chicken boullion cubes

1 tsp shichimi togarashi (Japanese mixed chili pepper spice), optional

Additional Toppings

½ head red cabbage, shredded (small mound per serving)

4 tsp fresh ginger, grated (1 tsp per serving)

4 green onions, chopped (1 tbsp per serving)

1 Pulse half of each of the mushrooms in a food processor until finely chopped; if you don't have a food processor, you can finely chop them by hand. The remaining mushrooms should be sliced and saved for topping.

2 Put aside the chopped mushrooms to add to your soup base later.

3 Boil a pot of water for your noodles. In a separate saucepan, combine 1½ cups (360 ml) Shio Base, 8 cups (1.8 L) chicken or vegetable stock, the heavy whipping cream, finely chopped mushroom mixture, chicken boullion, and shichimi togarashi to a boil then lower the heat and let simmer until you are ready to serve. Use about 2 cups (475 ml) soup per serving. Right before serving, crank it back up to a boil.

4 Boil the noodles—if fresh, boil for about 1 minute; if packaged, boil for about 2 minutes. As soon as they're done, drain well and separate into serving bowls.

5 Pour 2 cups (475 ml) soup over each bowl of noodles. Top each bowl with the remaining mushrooms, cabbage, a dollop of fresh ginger, green onions, and a marinated half-cooked egg.

Crispy Greens Ramen

LEVEL 2

Serves 6

Prep time:
30 minutes, plus time
to make Ramen Soup
Base, Ramen Noodles
(optional), Poached
Egg (optional),
and Garlic Chips
(optional)

I am a big fan of Swiss chard, kale, and Brussels sprouts but I love them even more when they are cooked crisp in the oven. They stay surprisingly crunchy in this ramen and even when they sink into the coconut-and-fish-sauce-infused Shio Base, the little nooks of the leaves fill with deliciousness and leave you so satisfied. The healthy greens really balance out the richness of the coconut milk.

To Make in Advance

Shio Base (page 10)
or your base of choice

Ramen Noodles
(page 13)

Poached Egg (page 21)

Garlic Chips (page 32)

1 small bunch Swiss chard, center vein removed and leaves chopped (I prefer rainbow chard)

1 small bunch kale, center vein removed and leaves chopped (I prefer dino kale)

10 Brussels sprouts, halved, thinly sliced

2 tbsp olive oil

Salt and pepper, to season

Add to Soup

1½ cups (360 ml) coconut milk

3 tsp fish sauce

Additional Toppings

6 green onions, chopped (1 tbsp per serving)

1 bunch cilantro, leaves only (small pile per serving)

1½ limes, quartered (1 quarter per serving)

1 Preheat the oven to 400°F (200°C). Put the rack in the middle position and line a baking sheet with parchment.

2 Wash and dry your Swiss chard and kale. Make sure there is no moisture left on the leaves.

3 Chop the Swiss chard, kale, and Brussels sprouts.

4 Toss your leaves with olive oil and sprinkle salt and pepper over. Place on baking sheet and bake for about 15 minutes or until crisp. Watch carefully to avoid burning. Remove and set aside.

5 Boil a pot of water for your noodles. In a separate saucepan, combine 2¼ cups (530 ml) Shio Base, 12 cups (1.8 L) vegetable or chicken stock, coconut milk, and fish sauce to a boil, then lower the

heat and let simmer until it's ready to serve. Note: It's 3 tablespoons of base to every 1 cup (235 ml) chicken or vegetable stock. Use about 2 cups (475 ml) soup per serving. Right before serving, crank it back up to a boil.

6 Boil the noodles—if fresh, boil for about 1 minute; if packaged, boil for about 2 minutes. As soon as they're done, drain well and separate into serving bowls.

7 Pour 2 cups (475 ml) soup over each bowl of noodles. Top with a mountain of crispy greens, green onions, cilantro, lime wedge, poached egg, and garlic chips.

Veggie Rainbow Ramen

LEVEL 1

Serves 6

**Prep time:
30 minutes, plus time
to make Ramen Soup
Base, Ramen Noodles
(optional), and
Menma (optional)**

*To Make in
Advance*

Shoyu Base (page 8)
or your base of choice

Ramen Noodles
(page 13)

Menma (page 20)

I love how this dish appeals to all the senses. The beautiful colors, the smell of the soup, the crunch of the fresh menma, the velvety quality of the quail eggs, the delicate taste of the shoyu seasoning—it's veggie heaven and tastes as good as it looks.

2 tbsp sesame oil

4 tbsp mirin (sweet rice wine)

2 garlic cloves, minced

2 tbsp grated ginger

6 tbsp shoyu (soy sauce)

1 red pepper, seeded and julienned

3 medium-sized carrots, shredded

1 cup (50 g) bean sprouts

1 cup (75 g) snap peas

¼ head Napa cabbage, shredded

¼ head red cabbage, shredded

Additional Toppings

12 raw quail eggs, optional (2 per serving)

3 tsp sesame seeds (I prefer black sesame seeds; ½ tsp per serving)

6 chives, chopped (I prefer garlic chives; small pile per serving)

1 Combine the sesame oil, mirin, garlic, ginger, and shoyu in the bottom of a wok or medium-sized frying pan. Heat to high.

2 Cook the vegetables for about 5 minutes in the wok or frying pan until cabbage wilts and the carrots are cooked through. Turn off the heat and set aside.

3 Boil a pot of water for your noodles. In a separate saucepan, bring 12 cups (2.8 L) Shoyu Base to a boil, then lower the heat and let simmer until you are ready to serve. Use about 2 cups (475 ml) soup per serving. Right before serving, crank it back up to a boil.

4 Boil the noodles—if fresh, boil for about 1 minute; if packaged, boil for about 2 minutes. As soon as they're done, drain well and separate into serving bowls.

5 Pour 2 cups (475 ml) soup over each bowl of noodles. Top with vegetable mixture, menma, and quail eggs. Garnish with sesame seeds and chives.

Cold Ramen

副菜

Cold Noodle Broth

LEVEL 1

Serves 6

Prep time: 30 minutes

My brother-in-law, Victor, got this recipe from his uncle who runs a small restaurant in Yokohama, Japan. The broth is very strong, so use it sparingly. It's more like a flavorful sauce than a soup, so don't over-serve this one. It's super simple and perfect for a nice hot day.

3½ cups (350 ml) water

1½ cups (150 g) sugar (I prefer baker's sugar as it's finer and dissolves quicker)

1½ cups (350 ml) mirin (rice wine vinegar)

½ cup (120 ml) shoyu (soy sauce)

Sesame oil

1   In a medium pot over medium-high heat, add the water, sugar, vinegar, and shoyu. Mix well until the sugar dissolves.

2   Remove from the heat and let cool before using the broth.

3   Right before serving, add a couple of drops of sesame oil to each serving. Serve over cold noodles with your toppings of choice.

Chilled Cucumber Tsukemen

LEVEL 1

Serves 4

Prep time: 20 minutes,
plus time to make
Cold Noodle Broth,
Ramen Noodles
(optional), and
Kakuni (optional)

Tsukemen refers to a dish of noodles that are served separately and dipped in a flavorful soup that coats the noodles and seasons every bite. It's not usually chilled, so this is my own version. It's light and refreshing and perfect for brunch or lunch. I love its vibrant color and gentle hint of mint.

2 lbs (900 g) cucumbers (2–3 cucumbers),
    peeled, seeded, and chopped, yielding
    4 cups (540 g)
2 yellow peppers, seeded and chopped
2 green onions, chopped
1 tbsp mint leaves
1½ tsp grated ginger
1 tsp salt
¼ tsp white pepper

Additional Toppings

1 cucumber, julienned (small bunch
    per serving)

To Make in Advance

Cold Noodle Broth
(page 114)

Ramen Noodles
(page 13)

Kakuni (page 28)

1 Boil a pot of water for your noodles. Boil the noodles—if fresh, boil for about 1 minute; if packaged, boil for about 2 minutes. As soon as they're done, drain well and refrigerate in a bath of cold water for at least 1 hour.

2 Combine the cucumbers, peppers, green onions, mint, and ginger in a blender. Add 2 cups (475 ml) of your cold noodle broth. Puree until very smooth and frothy.

3 Transfer the soup to the refrigerator and chill for at least 2 hours.

4 Season with salt and white pepper.

5 Serve the cold noodles with 1 cup (235 ml) of the cold soup per serving in a separate bowl. The noodles are for dipping into the cold soup. Add the julienned cucumber and sliced kakuni to top the noodles.

Hiyashi Chuka Ramen

LEVEL 1

Serves 6

Prep time: 20 minutes, plus time to make Cold Noodle Broth, Ramen Noodles (optional), Chashu (optional), and Beni Shoga (optional)

To Make in Advance

....

Cold Noodle Broth
(page 114)
....

Ramen Noodles
(page 13)
....

Chashu (page 22)
....

Beni Shoga (page 25)
....

Hiyashi Chuka Ramen means "Chilled Chinese Ramen," but as with many Chinese dishes, the Japanese have made their own version. This refreshing ramen-type salad with cold broth is normally served in the summer, with its colors speaking to what's in season. There are all kinds of variations of this, so feel free to substitute with what you have fresh on hand for your own version.

2 eggs

¼ tsp salt

½ tsp sugar

1 tsp vegetable oil

Additional Toppings

6 slices (170 g) Black Forest ham, julienned (1 slice/28 g per serving)

2 cups (100 g) bean sprouts (⅓ cup/17g per serving)

1 Japanese cucumber, seeded and julienned (¼ cup/25 g per serving)

3 medium-sized carrots, shredded (½ carrot per serving)

3 sheets nori (seaweed), julienned (½ sheet per serving)

Roasted sesame seeds, for garnish

1 Boil a pot of water for your noodles. Boil the noodles—if fresh, boil for about 1 minute; if packaged, boil for about 2 minutes. As soon as they're done, drain well and refrigerate in a bath of cold water for at least 1 hour.

2 Beat the eggs with the salt and sugar.

3 Heat the vegetable oil in a large skillet over medium heat. Pour the egg mixture into a pan and make a very thin omelet, like a crepe. Remove with a spatula and let cool. Roll up like a cigar and shred thinly with a knife.

4 Drain the cold noodles well and separate into serving bowls.

5 Pour 1 cup (235 ml) cold noodle broth over each bowl of chilled noodles. Top each bowl with eggs, ham, bean sprouts, cucumber, carrots, chashu, and a small amount of beni shoga. Garnish with roasted nori strips and sesame seeds.

Slow-Roasted Tomato and Miso Spinach Chilled Ramen

LEVEL 2

Serves 6

Prep time: 2½ hours, plus time to make Cold Noodle Broth, Ramen Noodles (optional), and Poached Egg

To Make in Advance

....
Cold Noodle Broth
(page 114)
....
Ramen Noodles
(page 13)
....
Poached Egg (page 21)
....

The tender and herb-laden slow-roasted tomatoes really are the star of this dish. The spinach is reminiscent of traditional Japanese *goma-ae*, made by coating spinach with sesame paste. These, coupled with a poached egg and the Cold Noodle Broth, make a rewarding lunch after a big morning workout.

½ cup (120 ml) olive oil

2 sprigs fresh rosemary, chopped

2 sprigs thyme, chopped

1 tsp salt

⅛ tsp white pepper

2½ lbs (1.1 kg) tomatoes, stems removed and halved horizontally

3 tsp sesame oil, divided

1 lb (455 g) baby spinach leaves, washed and dried

1 tbsp sesame paste or tahini

2 tbsp shoyu (soy sauce)

2 tbsp mirin (sweet rice wine)

Additional Toppings

2 cups (100 g) bean sprouts (⅓ cup/17 g per serving)

Roasted sesame seeds, for garnish

1   Preheat the oven to 325°F (170°C) with the rack set in the middle position. Combine the olive oil, rosemary, thyme, salt, and pepper in a shallow baking pan. Add the tomatoes and toss until well coated, laying them cut side down before cooking.

2   Roast the tomatoes for 2 hours or until they are completely wilted and soft.

3   While the tomatoes are roasting, boil a pot of water for your noodles. Boil the noodles—if fresh, boil for about 1 minute; if packaged, boil for about 2 minutes. As soon as they're done, drain well and refrigerate in a bath of cold water for at least 1 hour.

4   Cook the spinach in three batches. Heat 1 teaspoon sesame oil in a large skillet over medium-high heat. Add the spinach leaves and sauté, moving around frequently until just cooked, about a minute. Remove and set in a bowl. Repeat with additional batches. When the spinach cools, squeeze out any excess water.

5   In a small bowl, whisk the sesame paste, shoyu, and mirin until combined. Add the spinach and coat with sauce.

6   Drain the cold noodles well and separate into serving bowls.

7   Pour 2 cups (475 ml) cold noodle broth over each bowl of chilled noodles. Top each bowl with two roasted tomatoes, miso spinach, a mound of bean sprouts, and a poached egg. Garnish with roasted sesame seeds.

Specialty Ramen

スペシャルラーメン

Green Seaweed Fried Chicken Ramen

LEVEL 3

Serves 6

Prep time: 45 minutes, plus time to make Ramen Soup Base, Ramen Noodles (optional), and Marinated Half-Cooked Egg (optional)

To Make in Advance

....
Tonkotsu Base (page 5) or your base of choice
....
Ramen Noodles (page 13)
....
Marinated Half-Cooked Egg (page 26)
....

I recently discovered *aonoriko*, a powdered seaweed used to season soups and tempura and as a topping for *okonomiyaki* (a Japanese savory pancake). It's a fine powder and adds dark-green specks of flavor, turning an ordinary batter into something special. This recipe makes an aonoriko-battered chicken that I broil instead of deep-fry, so it's not only healthy but it takes on a dumpling-like quality that blends well with ramen.

4 tbsp cornstarch (I prefer katakuriko, or Japanese potato starch)

$3/4$ lb (340 g) boneless, skinless chicken thighs, cut into bite-sized pieces

Nonstick cooking spray

Batter

1 egg

½ cup (120 ml) cold water

½ cup (55 g) flour

1 tbsp aonoriko (Japanese powdered seaweed)

1 tsp salt

Additional Toppings

1 can baby corn (2–3 ears per serving)

1 bunch pea shoots (small pile per serving)

6 tsp grated ginger (1 tsp per serving)

1 lemon, sliced into 6 segments

1 Set the oven rack to 4–6 inches (10–15 cm) from the heating element and preheat the broiler.

2 Sprinkle the cornstarch over the chicken pieces.

3 In a separate bowl, whisk the egg, cold water, and flour together. Gently incorporate the aonoriko and salt into the batter without overmixing.

4 Line a cookie sheet with parchment paper and coat with cooking spray so that chicken doesn't stick.

5 Dip the chicken pieces into the batter and lay them on the cookie sheet so that they don't touch.

6 Broil for about 6 minutes, flip, then broil for an additional 5 minutes or until they start to brown around the edges. Watch closely so they do not burn, as ovens vary. They should resemble the texture of a dumpling.

7   Set the chicken on a wire rack to cool.

8   Boil a pot of water for your noodles. In a separate saucepan, bring 12 cups (1.8 L) Tonkotsu Base to a boil, then lower the heat and let simmer until you are ready to serve. Right before serving, crank it back up to a boil.

9   Boil the noodles—if fresh, boil for about 1 minute; if packaged, boil for about 2 minutes. As soon as they're done, drain well and separate into serving bowls.

10 Pour 2 cups (475 ml) soup over each bowl of noodles. Top each bowl with a couple pieces of chicken, some baby corn, a mound of spinach, and a marinated half-cooked egg. Garnish with a lemon segment to be squeezed over before eating.

Cheese Ramen

LEVEL 3

Serves 4

**Prep time:
30 minutes, plus
time to make Miso
and Tonkotsu Bases,
Ramen Noodles
(optional), Marinated
Half-Cooked Egg
(optional), and
Roasted Garlic
Butter (optional)**

*To Make in
Advance*

Tonkotsu Base (page 5)

Miso Base (page 3)

Ramen Noodles
(page 13)

Marinated Half-
Cooked Egg (page 26)

Roasted Garlic Butter
(page 31)

My friend Bradley, who often travels to Tokyo for business, insisted that I try his favorite cheese ramen shop, Tsukomo. They use a local artisan cheese called Golden Gouda that they grate paper-thin with a big machine that sits on the bar; then they place a huge mound of the cheese on the ramen. The finely shredded cheese melts right into every bite. This is my rendition of that delicious creation, but you must try the original if you are in Tokyo (page 159). This recipe is all in the prep, so once you have your major components made ahead of time, you really can throw this together very quickly.

1 cup (100 g) Brussels sprouts, outer leaves
   trimmed
2 tbsp olive oil (I prefer smoked olive oil)
½ tsp kosher salt
1 cup (235 ml) chicken stock
1 cup (100 g) finely grated aged Gouda cheese
   (use a microplane to get it very fine)

Additional Toppings

4 cups (400 g) finely grated aged Gouda cheese
   (1 cup/100g per serving)

1 Preheat the oven to 400°F (200°C). Put the rack in the middle position and line a baking sheet with parchment.
2 Toss your Brussels sprouts leaves with olive oil and sprinkle with kosher salt. Arrange them in a single layer so that they do not touch and bake for about 10 minutes or until crispy and brown around the edges. Watch carefully to avoid burning. Remove and set aside.
3 Boil a pot of water for your noodles.
4 Take your whole roasted bulb of garlic, if using, remove the cloves and smash them with the back of a knife to make a paste.

5 In a separate large saucepan, whisk 5 cups (1.1 L) Tonkotsu Soup and ¼ cup Miso Base with the (235 ml) chicken stock, roasted garlic paste, and grated Gouda cheese until well combined. Bring to a boil, then lower the heat and let simmer until you are ready to serve. Right before serving, crank it back up to a boil.

6 Boil the noodles—if fresh, boil for about 1 minute; if packaged, boil for about 2 minutes. As soon as they're done, drain well and separate into serving bowls.

7 Pour 1½ cups (360 ml) cheesy soup over each bowl of noodles. Top each bowl with a big pile of cheese, a similar pile of crispy Brussels sprouts, a marinated half-cooked egg, and a dollop of roasted garlic butter.

Kamo Matcha Ramen

LEVEL 3

Serves 4

Prep time: 30 minutes, plus time to marinate duck overnight, soak cedar plank for 1 hour, and make Ramen Soup Base, Ramen Noodles (optional), and Marinated Half-Cooked Egg (optional)

Equipment: Cedar plank presoaked in water for at least 1 hour

To Make in Advance

Shio Base (page 10) or your base of choice

Ramen Noodles (page 13)

Marinated Half-Cooked Egg (page 26)

This recipe was inspired by photos of a matcha-infused ramen posted on my friend Brian's *Ramen Adventures* blog. I was inspired to make a tea-smoked duck ramen with a matcha-fortified Shio Base. My cousin Brian and his friend Jace helped me test this one out and both of them said they'd never had anything like it, and that it was as delicious as it was unique. The recipe requires a cedar plank that can be purchased online or at most cooking stores. Cedar planks impart an intense, smoky flavor to the duck in a relatively short amount of time. I add liquid smoke to make it even stronger.

6 tsp matcha powder, divided

2 tbsp shoyu (soy sauce)

2 tbsp brown sugar

¼ tsp ground cinnamon

2 tbsp Shaoxing wine (you can substitute dry sherry)

2 tsp sesame oil

1 tbsp grated ginger

1 tsp minced garlic

1 tsp liquid smoke

2 duck breasts, skin on

Salt and pepper, to season

Broth

8 cups (1.8 L) chicken stock

½ cup or 1 stick (114 g) butter

8 tbsp mirin (sweet rice wine)

8 tsp wakame (you can substitute 1 tsp fish sauce)

8 dried shiitake mushrooms

Additional Toppings

1 pear, skin removed and sliced thin (3–4 slices per serving)

1 bunch Chinese cilantro, leaves only (small pile per serving)

1. In a small bowl, whisk 2 teaspoons of the matcha powder with the shoyu, brown sugar, cinnamon, dry sherry, sesame oil, ginger, garlic, and liquid smoke to make a marinade. Soak the duck breasts in the marinade, cover, and chill overnight.

2. Preheat the grill to medium-high heat.

3. Remove the duck from the marinade and cut it on the skin side with a sharp knife in a crosshatch pattern. Season both sides with salt and pepper. Save the marinade for later use.

4. Place the cedar plank on the grill on direct heat and cover until it starts to smoke. Turn the plank over and place on indirect heat.

5. Place the duck, skin side up, on the plank and cook for about 25 minutes, or until an internal thermometer pushed into the duck reads 165°F (74°C).

6. Remove the duck from the plank and set skin side down on direct heat to crisp the skin, or approximately 3–4 minutes. Remove and let rest.

7. Boil a pot of water for your noodles. In a separate large pot, start preparing the broth for your Shio Base. To your 8 cups (1.8 L) chicken stock, add the butter, mirin, wakame, and shiitake mushrooms and bring this to a boil. Then lower the heat and simmer for 10 minutes; strain out all solids.

8. To this stock, add 1½ cups (360 ml) of Shio Base. Then add the remaining marinade from your duck and 4 teaspoons matcha, leaving the soup a deep green color. Heat this back up to a boil, lower the heat and let simmer until ready to use. Right before serving, crank it back up to a boil.

9. Slice your duck on the bias and set aside.

10. Boil the noodles—if fresh, boil for about 1 minute; if packaged, boil for about 2 minutes. As soon as they're done, drain well and separate into serving bowls.

11. Pour 2 cups (475 ml) soup over each bowl of noodles. Top each bowl with ½ sliced duck per serving, sliced pear, some cilantro, and a marinated half-cooked egg.

Lobster Ramen

Although my husband and kids were great testers for my recipes, I figured I'd give them a break from ramen every night and invite friends over during the day to taste some of the really special ones. This one hit it out of the park—the lobster shell infused Shio Base is what did it for them. It was also very pleasing to the eye—with the shredded purple cabbage adding such beautiful color and the lemon zest giving a brightness to both the soup and the lobster. This is one of my favorites.

Serves 6

Prep time: 45 minutes, plus time to make Ramen Soup Base, Ramen Noodles (optional), and Roasted Garlic Butter (optional)

Equipment: Wooden skewers presoaked in water for at least 15 minutes

To Make in Advance

Shio Base (page 10)

Ramen Noodles (page 13)

Roasted Garlic Butter (page 31)

6 lobster tails, 5–6 oz (140–170 g) each

6 tbsp clarified butter (I prefer ghee)

Lobster Broth

12 cups (2.8 L) chicken or vegetable stock, homemade or store-bought

¾ cup or 1½ sticks (170 g) unsalted butter

¾ cup (175 ml) mirin (sweet rice wine)

1 large rectangular piece of kombu (about 10 inches/25 cm long), cut into large squares

12 dried shiitake mushrooms, crumbled into small pieces

6 bay leaves

Additional Toppings

½ head red cabbage, shredded (small mound per serving)

1 bunch arugula and spinach mixed (small mound per serving)

1½ lemons (¼ tsp zest and 1 quarter per serving)

1 Preheat oven to 450°F (230°C).

2 Split the lobster tails down the center of the back by turning over and cutting in half lengthwise through the shell with kitchen scissors, starting from the top and leaving the fin intact.

3 Thread a soaked skewer through the underside of the tail through the bottom of the shell.

4 Brush the underside portion with the exposed meat with clarified butter. Wrap in foil and set on a baking tray. Bake for 15 minutes. Remove the lobster tails from the foil and reserve the drippings.

5 Make the Lobster Broth: In a large soup pot over a high heat, combine the stock, butter, mirin, kombu, dried shiitake mushrooms, bay leaves, and reserved lobster drippings. Bring to a boil and reduce to a simmer.

6 Carefully remove the lobster meat from the shell by sliding a knife under the meat and gently lifting it out of its shell. Add the shells and the lobster juices to your stock. Cover and simmer for about 30 minutes.

7 Boil a pot of water for your noodles.

8 Line a colander with cheesecloth and set it over a pot large enough to hold the stock. Strain the lobster stock and return it to the stove. Add ³/₄ cup (180 ml) Shio Base. Right before serving, crank it back up to a boil.

9 Boil the noodles—if fresh, boil for about 1 minute; if packaged, boil for about 2 minutes. As soon as they're done, drain well and separate into serving bowls.

10 Pour 2 cups (475 ml) soup over each bowl of noodles. Top each bowl with a lobster tail, shredded purple cabbage, and a small mound of arugula and spinach mixed together. Add the lemon zest and a dollop of roasted garlic butter, and squeeze a lemon wedge over each bowl before serving.

Sides

副菜

Agedashi-Doufu Fried Tofu

LEVEL 2

Serves 4-6

Prep time: 20 minutes

When I ordered this in a restaurant, I couldn't understand how the tofu could stay crispy when it's swimming in sauce. I found out the trick here is to just lightly dust the tofu before frying it to achieve a delicate crispiness and still maintain a smooth and silky center. Too much batter makes it gummy. A daikon grater is essential here; try one and you'll see what a difference it makes.

2 blocks soft tofu

Vegetable oil, for frying

3 tbsp cornstarch (I prefer katakuriko, or Japanese potato starch)

Sauce

1 packet dashi granules (keep in packet form)

2 cups (475 ml) water

3 tbsp shoyu (soy sauce)

2 tsp mirin (sweet rice wine)

2 tbsp sake

Garnish

1 daikon, peeled and grated with excess liquid squeezed out

4-5 chives, chopped (I prefer garlic chives)

Bonito fish flakes, optional (1 tsp per serving)

1   Drain the tofu and wrap it carefully in a paper towel. Set it on a plate in the refrigerator for 20 minutes to get all of the moisture out. Remove, unwrap, and cut the tofu into small cubes, each piece being 1 inch (2.5 cm) in width.

2   In a small saucepan, combine the dashi, water, shoyu, mirin, and sake. Heat to boil, then turn down to a simmer and cover. Simmer for 10 minutes. Remove the dashi packet and keep covered on a low simmer until ready to use.

3   In a deep frying pan, add enough oil so that the tofu can completely submerge (about 1½ inches/ 4 cm). Heat on high to approximately 375°F (190°C), or when a small piece of the tofu sizzles immediately when added.

4   While the oil is heating, lightly dust the cornstarch onto the tofu so that it is completely covered on all sides. You can use a sieve to dust or make a little duster out of cheesecloth tied with baking string.

5   With a slotted spoon, gently lay the pieces of tofu into the hot oil, being careful not to overcrowd them. Cook in batches while rolling each piece over to cook on all sides. Remove when the tofu barely changes color and becomes crisp and almost inflated-looking. Do not brown. Set to drain on a paper towel.

6   Arrange a couple of spoonfuls of the sauce in a serving dish and lay a couple of pieces of your tofu in the sauce. Garnish with daikon, chives, and bonito fish flakes, if you like.

Basic Japanese Rice

LEVEL 1

**Makes as much
as you need**

**Prep time:
25 minutes**

Making fluffy and tender Japanese rice is a breeze if you have a rice cooker. I highly recommend treating yourself to one. Even the basic versions can keep your rice warm for days. How cool is that? If you don't have a rice cooker, no worries—making rice on the stove is pretty easy, too.

Japanese rice is shorter grained and higher in starch content than other rices, which gives it its stickier consistency. The rice needs to be washed multiple times to rinse off the surface starch and hydrate the grains. I actually prefer short-grain brown rice, which is cooked in the same manner. If you live near one, visit a Japanese market and you'll see different brands of Japanese rice that vary according to region, price, and quality—be adventurous and try them out. When you've had an excellent bowl of rice, you'll know.

2 cups (400 g) Japanese short-grain white rice*
1 qt or 4 cups (1 L) water

* *If you want to increase the amount of rice, add 2 cups (475 ml) additional water for every 1 cup (200 g) rice.*

If you don't have a rice cooker, follow these easy instructions for the stove top.

1 In a medium saucepan, add the raw rice and thoroughly rinse in the sink by pouring water over the rice until it is covered by about 2 inches (5 cm) of water. Swirl and squeeze the rice and water with your hands until the water looks milky.
2 Carefully pour out the milky water, leaving the rice. Repeat 3 times or until the water runs clear.
3 Once the water runs clear, give it a final drain. Cover the rice with 1 quart or 4 cups (1 L) water to begin cooking.
4 Place the lid on the pan and start cooking the rice on high until the water has come to a boil. Turn the heat down to just above a simmer and cook for 20 minutes (brown rice may require more cooking time). Do not remove the lid when cooking as steam will be released, extending the cooking time. Remove from heat and let steam with the lid on for an additional 10 minutes before serving. Results should be perfect!

Chahan Fried Rice

LEVEL 1

Serves 8

Prep time: 20 minutes, plus time to make Basic Japanese Rice

To Make in Advance

....

Basic Japanese Rice (page 138)

....

In Japan, you'll often see fried rice offered on the menu at ramen shops alongside fried dumplings. In my home growing up, we ate fried rice for breakfast. My own recipe has changed over the years but this is a basic one that you can add almost anything to. The options are endless, so experiment to make your own rendition: make it pork-free; throw in some chopped pineapple for a Hawaiian version; or use up those vegetables you didn't finish last night. If you are making it for your kiddos, skip the sriracha.

4 strips bacon

¼ red onion, finely chopped

1 tbsp sesame oil

4 cups (745 g) cooked Basic Japanese Rice

2 eggs

2 tbsp shoyu (soy sauce)

1 tsp sriracha (optional)

1 In a medium- to large-sized skillet, cook 4 strips of bacon until well done. Set aside on a paper towel and crumble when cooled. Do not discard your bacon grease.

2 In the pan with leftover bacon grease, sauté the onions on medium-high heat until they start to brown, stirring frequently for 2 minutes.

3 Add the sesame oil to the onions.

4 Immediately add the rice and incorporate until it is coated with the grease, oil, and onions. The rice will start to make a popping sound as it gets crispy.

5 Make a well in the middle of the rice and crack the eggs into it. Take a fork or chopsticks and mix the eggs up in the middle.

6 Combine the egg and rice mixture until the eggs cook through—you'll be able to see little pieces of cooked egg throughout as it completely cooks.

7 Add the shoyu and Sriracha, if using, and mix through.

8 Mix in the crumbled bacon right before serving to preserve its crispiness and serve warm.

Sweet Pork Gohan (Rice)

LEVEL 1

Serves 6

Prep time: 30 minutes,
plus time to make
Basic Japanese Rice

To Make in Advance

....

Basic Japanese Rice
(page 138)

....

This recipe was inspired by one from my blogger friend Brian, at Ramen Adventures. He had just returned from Hiroshima where they were in the midst of a soupless tantanmen (Japanese version of a spicy Chinese-style ramen) boom. When you finish the noodles, there is a sludge of tare (highly packed flavoring base), ground pork, and green onions left in the bowl, to which you are meant to add rice. This is a very simplified, non-spicy variation but feel free to add a spicier kick if you'd like.

½ onion
1 carrot, peeled and cut into thirds
1 tbsp sesame oil
1 lb (455 g) ground pork
2 tbsp shoyu (soy sauce)
2 tbsp sugar
1 tbsp sake
1 tsp ginger
6 cups (1.1 kg) cooked Basic Japanese Rice
3 green onions, chopped, for garnish

1   Pulse the onion and carrot in a food processor until finely chopped, or chop finely by hand.
2   Heat the sesame oil in a large skillet on medium-high heat. Add the onion and carrot mixture and sauté until the onions are translucent—about 10 minutes.
3   Add the ground pork to the skillet with the vegetables and cook through until no longer pink. Lower the heat to a simmer.
4   In a small bowl, whisk the shoyu, sugar, sake, and ginger until well combined.
5   Pour the sauce over the pork and incorporate.
6   Take the mixture and put back into food processor to pulse until you get a fine consistency. Alternatively, you can use an immersion blender in the pan to pulse.
7   To serve, prepare a bowl of warm rice and ladle a generous portion of the sweet pork over the top. Garnish with chopped green onion.

Cucumber Sunomono (Salad)

LEVEL 3

Serves 4–6

Prep time: 20 minutes, plus 1 hour to chill

This light and refreshing salad is the perfect accompaniment to a rich and filling bowl of ramen. The trick to making the cucumbers soak up all of the delicious dressing is to cut them wafer-thin. An inexpensive, plastic, Japanese mandoline slicer is the tool for the job and well worth the minimal investment.

2 cucumbers (I prefer Japanese or English cucumbers)

¼ tsp salt, plus additional to season

1 tsp dried wakame (optional)

½ cup (100 g) sugar

½ cup (120 ml) Japanese rice vinegar

1 tsp shoyu (soy sauce)

Additional Toppings

Freshly cracked crab (optional)

Cooked baby shrimp (optional)

Chopped octopus (optional)

1   Slice the cucumber with a mandoline on the lowest setting for a very thin cut. Put in a bowl and sprinkle with salt, incorporate, and set aside. This will help get all of the water out of the cucumber so that the salad is not soggy.

2   Soak the wakame in water for about 10 minutes. Squeeze out all excess water and julienne into thin strips. Whisk together the sugar, vinegar, ¼ teaspoon salt, and shoyu. Add the wakame.

3   Place the salted cucumbers in a colander and rinse with cold water. Squeeze out the excess water from the cucumbers and add to the vinegar mixture.

4   Chill for at least 1 hour before serving. If desired, top with freshly cracked crab, cooked baby shrimp, or chopped octopus.

Auntie Mary Jane's Cauliflower no Tsukemono (Pickled Vegetables)

LEVEL 1

My Auntie Mary Jane is a great cook and her pickled vegetables make an ideal side dish for ramen—the tartness of the vinegar brine complements a rich ramen soup.

Serves 10

Prep time: 30 minutes

1 head cauliflower, broken into bite-sized pieces
1 small onion, sliced (I prefer Vidalia)
1 carrot, sliced
3–4 ribs of celery, sliced
1 tsp red pepper flakes

Brine

1 cup (235 ml) white vinegar
1 cup (200 g) sugar
3 cups (700 g) water
4 tbsp kosher salt

1   Prepare an ice bath. Cut your vegetables and blanch your cauliflower, onion, and carrot in a pot of boiling water in separate batches for 30 seconds each. Return the water to a boil for each batch. Remove the vegetables and plunge into an ice bath. Set the celery aside.

2   Heat brine ingredients—the vinegar, sugar, water, and salt—in a medium pot on a high heat. Bring to a boil for 3 minutes or until the sugar dissolves, stirring frequently. Remove from the heat and cool to room temperature.

3   Put all of your vegetables in a container or glassware that can be covered. Pour the cooled brine mixture over the vegetables and refrigerate for at least 8 hours until ready to serve. Will keep for one week in a refrigerated airtight container.

Kim Family Potato Salad

LEVEL 1

Serves 6–8

Prep time: 35 minutes

My wonderful Korean friend, Soo, gave me this recipe. You'll find potato salad in bento boxes all over Japan. I enjoy it as a chilled side dish to complement a bowl of cold ramen in the summer. This one has a sweet crunch from the apples balanced with a bright zest from the gherkins and relish. For this recipe, the order that you add your ingredients is important. The apples are added at the end so they don't brown and the Parmesan is added after the potatoes so that the cheese can melt into the mixture. Thank you, Kim family, for sharing your secrets.

2 tsp salt, divided

3 medium russet potatoes, peeled and halved

3 eggs

3 slices pancetta, diced

½ cup (80 g) red onion, diced

½ cucumber, halved lengthwise, seeds removed, and thinly sliced (English cucumber preferred)

3 gherkins, halved lengthwise and thinly sliced

1 carrot, shredded

3 apples, cut into bite-sized pieces (I prefer Honeycrisp or Fuji, but any sweet variety works)

½ cup (40 g) Parmesan cheese, shredded

¾ cup (175 g) mayonnaise

¼ cup (60 g) sweet pickle relish

3 tbsp mustard (I prefer grainy mustard)

½ tsp pepper

1 Boil a large pot of water for your potatoes, and add about 1 teaspoon of salt to the water. Add your potatoes and boil for about 25 minutes, or until a knife can cut through them easily.

2 While the potatoes are boiling, place your eggs into a separate pot of cold water, fully covering them. Bring to a boil, and then immediately remove from the heat and cover. Let the eggs sit in the hot water for 10 minutes. Place in an ice bath for 3 minutes, crack, and peel. Cut the eggs into bite-sized pieces, yolk included. Add to a large bowl, big enough to mix all of your ingredients without being crowded.

3 Add the pancetta, red onion, cucumber, gherkins, and carrot to the bowl.

4 Drain the potatoes and set aside to cool. When cool, cut them into bite-sized pieces. Add to the bowl with the apples and the Parmesan.

5 Add the mayonnaise, relish, mustard, salt, and pepper, and mix all ingredients until well incorporated.

6 Refrigerate and serve cold. Will keep for 3 days.

Gyuniku Korokke (Beef and Potato Croquette) with Katsu Sauce

LEVEL 2

Makes 20 croquettes

Prep time: 1 hour

I never refuse the offer of a *korokke*. It is one of my favorite Japanese comfort foods. I love the super-crisp coating and their smooth, fluffy potato filling. The katsu sauce that you dip it in provides the zing that brings it all together.

1 tsp salt, plus additional to season

4 medium potatoes, peeled and quartered

2 tbsp olive oil

½ onion, diced

½ lb (225 g) ground beef

¼ cup (60 g) heavy whipping cream

2 tbsp sugar

2 tbsp shoyu (soy sauce)

Pepper, to season

4 eggs

2 tablespoons water

½ cup (55 g) flour (I prefer wheat flour)

4 cups (460 g) panko breadcrumbs

Vegetable oil, for frying

Katsu Sauce (can also substitute store-bought sauce)

¼ cup (60 g) ketchup (I prefer low-sodium)

1 tbsp shoyu (soy sauce)

1 tsp Worcestershire sauce

1 Boil a large pot of water with 1 teaspoon salt. Add the potatoes and cook for about 30 minutes or until a knife can cut through them easily.

2 In a large sauté pan on medium-high, add the olive oil. When heated, add the onion and cook until translucent. Add the beef and cook through, making sure to break up the beef into very small pieces. Set aside.

3 Drain the potatoes and use a potato ricer or masher to mash them in a large bowl.

4   Add the beef and onion mixture to the potatoes, and then pour over the whipping cream, sugar, shoyu, and a liberal sprinkling of salt and pepper. Combine well until mixture is ready to make small patties.

5   Prepare the Katsu sauce by combining the ketchup, shoyu, and Worcestershire sauce in a small bowl. Whisk together until incorporated.

6   Prepare a dipping station with the eggs beaten with a little water, flour, and breadcrumbs. Dip each croquette in egg, then flour, then egg again, then the breadcrumbs. Repeat for each croquette. You can freeze any croquettes you are not using in a freezer-safe container for up to 1 month.

7   Heat the oil on medium-high in the same sauté pan used before; use about ½-inch (6 mm) deep or half the width of a croquette. The oil will be ready when a pinch of breadcrumbs fries up quickly. Don't overcrowd the pan, fry 3–4 croquettes at a time.

8   Remove the croquettes and set onto a wire rack, do not let them touch.

9   Serve warm and drizzle some Katsu sauce over the top.

Auntie Betty's Shrimp Gyoza

LEVEL 2

Makes 30

Prep time: 1 hour

My Auntie Betty is a legendary cook in our family. She gets a special Dace fish paste from May Wah supermarket in the Richmond District of San Francisco. If you're ever in the area, grab some to make your gyoza just like hers. My auntie's inspiration came from a little restaurant in San Francisco that used to make the most delicious gyoza. The owner gave her the recipe without any real measurements, but through trial and error, she perfected it. Enjoy!

30 raw shrimp, peeled, deveined, and cleaned
½ cup (125 g) fish paste (I prefer Dace fish paste)
¼ cup (62.5 g) dried dill
1 large garlic clove, minced
1 tbsp unsalted butter, melted
2 tbsp heavy cream
1 tsp white pepper
1 package round won ton wrappers
4 tbsp vegetable oil
⅛ cup (30 ml) chicken stock

Dipping Sauce

½ cup (120 ml) shoyu (soy sauce)
¼ cup (60 ml) white vinegar
5 drops chili oil

1   Cut each shrimp into 3–4 small ½-inch (6 mm) pieces.
2   Combine the shrimp, fish paste, dill, garlic, butter, cream, and pepper in a medium bowl.
3   Drop the shrimp mixture by spoonful onto won ton rounds. Fold over and use hot water with your finger around half the round and fold over to seal.
4   Line a baking sheet with aluminum foil and lay the wontons in a row—it's fine if they are touching each other. If you want to serve them at a later date, freeze on an unlined baking sheet overnight, then transfer to a sealed bag to store.
5   Prepare the sauce by whisking the shoyu, vinegar, and chili oil until combined.
6   Heat the vegetable oil in a large skillet over medium-high heat. Brown the gyoza on both sides. Do not crowd the pan. Pour the chicken stock in the pan, cover, and let simmer for 4 minutes. Remove and serve with the sauce.

Crispy Teriyaki Chicken Wings

LEVEL 2

Makes 40 wings

Prep time: 1 hour

I don't normally serve fried food to my kids and I really tried to make this recipe by baking or broiling, but I just couldn't get the same crispiness for my mom's wings without resorting to a big 'ole pan of oil. We make these once a year for New Year's, so it's a special treat for all of us, but they are also great as a side dish with ramen. Warning: they are extremely addictive!

2 cups (475 ml) vegetable oil or enough to fill a medium-sized, deep saucepan about 1½ inches (4 cm)

1 cup (110 g) flour

1 cup (235 ml) water

3 ice cubes

2½ lbs (1.1 kg) chicken wings, washed and towel-dried

Sauce

1 cup (200 g) sugar

1 cup (235 ml) shoyu (soy sauce)

2 tsp grated ginger

¼ cup (60 ml) mirin (sweet rice wine)

1 Heat the sauce ingredients in a small saucepan to a boil and then turn down to simmer and leave it.

2 Prepare a wire rack on an aluminum foil-lined cookie sheet ready for the cooked chicken.

3 Heat the oil to medium-high in a deep saucepan.

4 Combine the flour and water to make batter. Add the ice cubes to the batter to keep cold, continuing to mix as the ice melts.

5 Test the oil by adding a very small amount of batter to the hot oil to see if it fries up quickly. If it does, your oil is ready.

6 Add the chicken wings to the batter in batches so that none are touching.

7 Fry in batches until both sides are brown and crispy; turn with metal tongs halfway through.

8 Dip the fried chicken wings in the simmering sauce for about 5 seconds.

9 Remove and drain on the prepared wire rack, making sure that the wings do not touch each other. This will maintain their crispiness. Serve hot or at room temperature.

Cousin Jilly's Pan Chirashizushi Dynamite

LEVEL 3

Serves 4–6

Prep time: 1 hour

Chirashizushi, or scattered sushi, is traditionally made by scattering raw fish and vegetables over sushi rice. This variation made by my cousin Jill mixes the ingredients into the rice and is topped with a crab dynamite mixture similar to those found on top of sushi that bakes up golden brown and is simply delicious. It's filling, so it's best to serve alongside a lighter-style ramen base such as Shio or Shoyu. It's great for parties, too, as it can be served hot or cold. Thanks, Jilly-Bean!

3 cups (585 g) Japanese rice, uncooked

1 large rectangular piece of kombu (about 10 inches/25 cm long), cut into large squares

3¼ cups (770 ml) water

⅓ cup (80 ml) rice wine vinegar

⅓ cup (65 g), plus 1 tbsp sugar, divided

1 tsp salt

2 eggs

2 tbsp vegetable oil, divided

2 tbsp shoyu (soy sauce)

½ lotus root, peeled, halved, and finely sliced

2 medium-sized carrots, peeled and shredded

¼ cup Nori Komi Furikake (available at most Asian markets or online)

5 shiitake mushrooms, cut into ¼-inch (6 mm) dice

½ onion, diced

1 cup (135 g) cooked crab meat

¾ cup (175 g) mayonnaise

¾ cup (175 g) sour cream

1 Preheat the oven to 350°F (180°C) with the rack in the middle position.

2 In a large pot or a rice cooker, rinse and drain the rice to remove impurities. Do this three or four times or until the water runs clear. Add the kombu and cover with the 3¼ cups (770 ml) fresh water. Let soak for 30 minutes. If you have a rice cooker, transfer the rice to it and follow the instructions. If you don't, cook your pot on high heat with the lid on. After the water has been boiling for 30 seconds, turn the heat down to simmer and continue to cook for 14–15 minutes. Briefly turn up the heat again, then remove from heat. Without removing the lid, allow the rice to steam for about 10 minutes.

3 In a small saucepan, whisk the rice wine vinegar, ⅓ cup (65 g) sugar, and salt. Bring to a boil, stirring often until the sugar dissolves. Remove from the heat.

4 In a small bowl, whisk the eggs. Heat 1 tablespoon vegetable oil in a saucepan over medium-high heat. Add the eggs in two separate batches and make two flat, thin omelets. Cool, roll up, and julienne.

5 Heat the shoyu and 1 tablespoon of sugar in a saucepan over medium-high heat. Add the lotus root and carrots and sauté until there is no more liquid in the pan, approximately 5 minutes. Set aside.

6 When the rice is done, quickly empty it into a large bowl and remove the kombu. Add the vinegar mixture, folding it in until the rice cools.

7 Add the julienned eggs from step 4 and the sautéed vegetables from step 5 into the rice and mix. Press into a 9 × 13-inch (23 × 33 cm) baking dish.

8 Sprinkle furikake on top.

9 Heat 1 tablespoon vegetable oil in a saucepan over medium-high heat. Add the mushrooms and onion and sauté until translucent, about 5 minutes.

10 In a medium bowl, combine the mushrooms, onion, crab, mayonnaise, and sour cream. Layer on top of the rice.

11 Bake for 25 minutes or until the top is golden brown. Let cool before cutting into small rectangles. To serve cold, refrigerate overnight and cut before serving. Serve alongside Cucumber Sunomono (page 141) and Roasted Nori (page 24) or on its own.

Mike's Arare (Japanese Rice Cracker Snack)

LEVEL 1

Serves 10–12
Prep time: 1½ hours

This is a Japanese-American rendition of *arare*—a rice-cracker snack seasoned with soy sauce. My brother's brother-in-law Mike's recipe is hands down the best. He was inspired by his wife, Mary, who wanted him to learn how to make it. It's everything you want in a snack: salty, sweet, and crispy. One handful and you're hooked.

1 cup or 2 sticks (225 g) butter
¾ cup (175 ml) corn syrup
2 tsp shoyu (soy sauce)
¾ cup (175 ml) vegetable oil
1 cup (200 g) baking sugar
2 boxes of Rice Chex cereal
2 bottles (3.4 oz/100 g) furikake (available at
    most Asian markets or online)

1   Preheat the oven to 250°F (120°C).
2   In a medium saucepan on medium-high heat, combine the butter, corn syrup, shoyu, and oil until the butter is melted.
3   Lower the heat and whisk in the sugar until dissolved. It should be the color of butterscotch and have a creamy texture. You should have a total of 3 cups (700 ml).
4   Pour one box of cereal each into two large tin-foil pans or roasting pans.
5   Add 1½ cups (360 ml) or half of the mixture over each pan of cereal, mixing well until the cereal is lightly coated.
6   Pour 1 bottle of furikake over each pan. Mix well.
7   Bake for 1 hour, mixing and turning over cereal mixture every 15 minutes.
8   Let cool before serving so that the cereal can get crispy.

Rameducate Yourself

It wasn't very long ago that as far as most Americans were concerned, ramen was a block of dried noodles that was sold in a plastic package with a tiny envelope of mysterious seasonings, and wasn't found much outside of college dorm rooms and the ateliers of starving artists. This "instant ramen" was developed by Momofuku Ando, a Taiwanese-Japanese businessman as a way to deal with post–World War II food shortages. It's only in the past decade that most Americans, including myself, have learned about the more traditional-style ramen made with long-simmered broths and artisan noodles that even appear on the menus of four-star restaurants.

My own ramen education took me from watching *Tampopo*, the classic movie about the Japanese love of food and search for the perfect noodle, directed by filmmaker Juzo Itami, to a more hands on one in Japan. While there, I enrolled in an intensive ramen-cooking course and toured the ramen shops of Tokyo with one of the city's best-known ramen bloggers (see page 156). Not only did I immerse myself in the culture of ramen, but I also learned a lot about myself as a Japanese-American.

The build-up to the trip included both excitement and trepidation. I am a *yonsei*, or fourth-generation Japanese-American, and this was my first visit to my ancestral homeland. I don't speak Japanese and I was worried about how people would treat me. I was told by relatives here in the United States to just speak English because the Japanese would rather not have you botch up their language; but if I was *hakujin*, or Caucasian, trying to speak Japanese then that would seem endearing. Weird. So, that's how I started, by speaking English and being a good *gaijin*, or foreigner. Then my ten years of Japanese school started kicking in, and every so often, I would try to say something in the native language. To my surprise, my garbled version of Japanese, or "Janglish," was met with overwhelming hospitality and patience. Being a yonsei seemed to inspire the locals to take me under their wings, knowing that I was Japanese—however long ago my ancestors lived there. It turned out to be an asset.

I was eager to get home and incorporate my newfound wisdom into my recipes. Sensei Rikisai at the Miyajima Ramen School in Osaka taught me that ramen was introduced to Japan at the end of the Edo Era in the late nineteenth century when the country finally allowed visitors. Before that, the country had been formally closed to all foreigners. The Chinese came and introduced the noodle, *lamien*. The Japanese quickly changed the name to *ramen* and sold it as street food. Around this same time, the Portuguese brought over a wind instrument called a *shawm*. The Japanese adapted it into what they call a *charumera*, which was used by the ramen sellers to signal buyers to their carts, in the way that an ice cream truck plays a tune when it drives down the block. Ramen's popularity began.

I was lucky to have Brian MacDuckston, an American living in Tokyo who blogs about his favorite food at *Ramen Adventures*, as my guide to the *ramen-yas* of Tokyo. He's just completed a ramen guide for exploring fifty of the best ramen shops in Tokyo and anyone traveling there with a hankering for ramen should consider this guide a must-have. I asked him for a brief summary of the current state of ramen in Tokyo. Here's what he had to say:

When the dish that would come to be known as ramen made its way from China to Japan, it was quite simple: noodles with a firm bite and a light broth, really meant only to keep the noodles hot and add a bit of flavor. It was easy to prepare in large quantities, quick to cook the noodles, and was well suited to feeding many people in a short amount of time. Burgers and fried chicken may be commonplace in modern Japan, but in the past one hundred years, ramen was the ultimate fast food.

It wasn't long before moms were cooking ramen at home. With the advent of modern preservatives, the home-cooked ramen family meal could be as easy as a big pot of instant noodles, or as complex as handmade everything—soup from scratch topped with the family's secret-recipe *chashu*. Most home meals lay somewhere in the middle—fresh noodles from the local noodle shop, a light chicken stock kicked up with umami-rich ingredients, and some roasted meats sourced from a nearby butcher. This was dinner for many modern Japanese families, and the effect of the past few decades are being felt around the world today.

For many who grew up in Japan, ramen is deeply nostalgic. Slurping is probably the most fun way to consume food, and ramen doesn't just encourage slurping, it practically requires it. So with the current generation of adults longing for their favorite childhood food, ramen shops have had to take things further. Known in Japanese as *kodawari*, chefs are paying extreme consideration to details. They'll use soy sauce blends made from tiny craft breweries, salt flown in from around the world, and chickens that are fed peculiar diets of wild sesame and mushrooms to give their egg yolks more flavor. This trend of kodawari means some amazing yet still relatively basic bowls of ramen.

If slurping alone isn't nostalgic enough, local varieties of ramen do even more to instill a sense of hometown. Some, such as Hokkaido's famous miso ramen, use locally sourced ingredients, such as miso, corn, and rich butter, to recall the flavors of the far north. Other areas, such as Hakata with their thick pork tonkotsu ramen, are more about the style. Hakata is home to hundreds of late night *yatai*, or street stalls, that sell stinky, porky, delicious ramen well

into the night. Other styles, such as Kitakata ramen, seem to mirror the simple countryside life. Kitakata ramen is light enough to eat for breakfast, an activity enjoyed by many before heading off to work in the rice fields.

With the kodawari boom, many home cooks have been able to experiment with customizing their bowls. The Internet means that specialty ingredients are just a click away. It is these extras—high quality kodawari ingredients and local flair—that have elevated ramen from a simple noodle soup to the gourmet level that it stands at today.

As you explore the world of ramen, you'll see how this regionality plays in the different soup bases and styles. Sensei Rikisai taught me that ramen is made up of three building blocks: a stock that is the base for everything; a small amount of *tare*, or a highly packed flavoring base, that is added to the stock to determine what type of ramen it is; and a fat that makes everything milder and balances the flavors out. Tare, when used as an adjective, becomes *dare*, as in *shiodare*, or strong salt flavor component. He described it as a perfectly staged play with each component having its own necessary role. With the exception of my Tonkotsu recipe (see page 5), which Sensei Rikisai taught me to make traditionally, I've simplified my other recipes and combined some of these building blocks to make it easier for the home cook.

The four main types of ramen that can be intermixed and changed by the stock, the tare, and type of fat added are Miso (miso paste blended in), Shio (a light salt component), Shoyu (mainly soy-sauce based), and Tonkotsu (creamy pork soup). The only thing that's a bit confusing is that Tonkotsu is a soup on its own, so you might see a Spicy Misodare Tonkotsu Soup, which is a combination of a Spicy Miso as the strong flavor component and Tonkotsu Soup. And a good soup has to have umami. My cooking course taught me that there are three kinds of umami: *glutamic acid umami*, which comes from ingredients such as seaweed and chicken; *isocyanic acid umami*, which comes from ingredients such as dried fish and mackerel; and *guanylic acid umami*, which comes from ingredients such as shiitake mushrooms and pork. Believe it or not, umami is very scientific—it's not just the fifth flavor sense that no one can describe.

Aside from the umami factor, the texture of the noodles is vital to a good bowl of ramen. Noodles can be made with varying levels of gluten. To understand this, for instance, a baguette has a medium-high level of gluten, whereas tempura, sweets, and cookies are low in gluten. Ramen noodles are in the semi-high gluten category. Most ramen chefs mix up the types of flours they use in their ramen noodles to experiment with these gluten levels. I use a combination of bread flour, cake flour, and wheat flour because I think it makes a lighter noodle. You can also vary the percentage of water mixed with "baked baking soda" or *kansui* powder (see page 14) to make a noodle that has a certain density. Noodles can be skinny, fat, flat, etc.—there isn't really a perfect formula. I use a 25 percent water to flour ratio in my recipe, but that's just what I think gives the best results for the mix of flours I am using.

Ramen is special because it's not just noodles and soup. It's a well-choreographed bowl of goodness, with each element able to stand out on its own. The time it takes to eat a bowl of ramen versus the time it takes to prepare it is completely disproportionate, another reason that makes this dish so intriguing. On your ramen path, you may want to seek out top-notch quality ramen by artisanal ramen masters who cultivate their own style. They'll have secret variations in the way they incorporate these components, and you'll start to recognize the differences the more you learn. What makes a good bowl for you may be a thick, rich Tonkotsu, or you might prefer a lighter Shio. That's why ramen can please the most finicky of noodle freaks.

What are the characteristics of a *good bowl*? The perfect density of soup brimming with depth and layered flavor; salt content that's not overpowering; handmade noodles that are firm yet springy, and hold up to the soup; and fresh toppings that have been given as much attention as everything else. A good bowl will give both your mind and body overall satisfaction and let you feel it for hours after as you lick your lips and still taste the soup lingering. Hungry yet?

Ramen Tour of Tokyo

Want to try the real deal in Tokyo, Japan? Brian MacDuckston, my colleague from *Ramen Adventures*, chaperoned me along with my friends Margret and Andi to these six ramen-yas, which I highly recommend for a nice, well-rounded tour to experience the different types of ramen available in Tokyo.

Most Tokyo ramen-yas have very minimal seating, with seats at a bar and no waiting area. The chef is always present and is typically only accompanied by one or two apprentices, depending on the size of the shop. And it's quiet. The Japanese like to face the chef and eat without talking or socializing. It is the same at sporting events or concerts in Japan; people stand side by side but there isn't much interaction as they enjoy the show. It is their way of showing respect to the performer, and to the master and his expertise at a ramen-ya.

Customers respect the line and wait without complaining—no looking at their phones or talking too much. They place their orders and pay at a small ticket machine at the front of the shop, and then line up outside, and sometimes along the back wall of the restaurant, as their turn draws closer. When a seat opens up, they are prompted. They sit down quickly, hand over their tickets, and wait for their ramen. Within minutes, the bowl is presented on a raised bar in front of them. They dig into their ramen and finish within 15 minutes. With a polite *"gochisosama,"* they exit and the next person sits. This efficient system keeps the line moving quickly.

Some ramen-yas are set up in more of a restaurant-style with a waiter, a menu, and proper drink service. You are welcome to stay longer at these establishments but my advice is to show respect and do as others do. Eat, enjoy, and get out. You can talk later.

Japanese Soba Noodles Tsuta, Master Onishi-san

Tokyo, Toshima-ku, Sugamo 1-14-1
Closest station: Sugamo
Open 11 a.m.–4 p.m.
Closed Tuesdays and Wednesdays

This was our first ramen stop in Tokyo and probably the most formal of all of the ramen-yas we went to. It had a long line at 11 a.m.; it was the first time we used the ticket machine to place an order, and everyone was quiet as a mouse, except for the slurping, of course. We were advised by Brian to only take pictures of the ramen, but to do this very quickly. Our bowls were placed on the raised bar and it was as if we were paying homage by reaching for it with both hands and placing it in front of us to consume. My traveling partner and photographer for the trip, Andi, and I each shared the Shoyu and Shio varieties and thought they were divine. The soup wasn't too heavy so we were able to finish them both, the egg filled with liquid gold and just enough negi (green onion) and chashu. The Shio version had a delicious green pesto-type topping that I think was made with *aonori*, a powdered seaweed.

LaShowHan, Master Okada-san

Tokyo, Chioda-ku, Kanda Nishikicho 1-4-8
Closest station: Ogawamachi
Open 11 a.m.–3 p.m., 5:30 p.m.–8 p.m.
Saturdays 11 a.m.–2 p.m., 5:30 p.m.–8 p.m.
Closed Sundays

This was my first taste of tantanmen, a Japanese adaptation of a Szechuan-style spicy noodle dish known as Dan Dan noodles. I don't tend to like super-spicy food, but the Premium Si Chuan–style bowl was not too overpowering, and the *sansho* pepper gave it an earthy, lemony taste that just slightly numbed my tongue. I loved that it was served *mazemen*-style (or without soup), so that the spices and the sauce were folded into every bite. I was just as fond of the owner, Master Okada-san. It's also not a strict sit, eat, and get out establishment, which was refreshing!

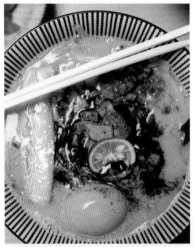

Mensho Tokyo, Master Shono-san

Yubinbango112-0003 Bunkyo-ku, Tokyo Kasuga 1-15-9 1F

Closest Station: Kasuga

Hours 11 a.m.–3 p.m., 5 p.m.–11 p.m.

Closed Tuesdays

Website: menya-shono.com/tokyo/access/

I ordered the Shoyu-Niboshitare Tonkotsu ramen with a side of tender lamb. The Tonkotsu is cooked with pork and lamb bones with a lamb chashu and the most interesting prep of menma in long strips to top it off. My favorite part was Master Shono-san's signature spice mix of ground cinnamon, cumin, and fennel seeds that was provided in a shaker at the table. The décor and ambience are cool and casual—he has a chandelier made out of *niboshi*, or dried infant sardines, in the front of the restaurant. He also has five other ramen shops in Tokyo, with one U.S. location in San Francisco.

Fuunji, Master Miyake-san

Hokuto first 2-14-3 1F, Yoyogi, Shibuya-ku, Tokyo

Closest station: Shinjuku

Hours 11 a.m.–3 p.m., 5 p.m.–9 p.m.

Closed Sundays

I read about this place on ramenadventures.com before my trip and was so excited to taste their *tsukemen*, or dipping noodles, with Brian himself. Unfortunately, he had another appointment to go to and couldn't stay for the whole experience, but he made sure we purchased the right ticket at the machine in the back and ushered us in. It was worth the wait—a complex and layered chicken-bone soup with deep fish flavors and an intensity that made every noodle-laden bite satisfying. Brian would later tell me that the soup is actually a *tori paitan*, with chicken bones cooked in the same way you would cook pork bones for a similar soup. It is then added to a second fish soup to give it that smoky flavor. Here the line continued to the back of the bar, where everyone watched over the customers in anticipation as seats would free up and our line slowly moved ahead. The master was super serious, very concentrated, and intently involved in his preparation for us. I was mesmerized.

Tsukomo, Master Takahashi-san

Hongoku Build. 1F, 1-1-36 Hiroo, Shibuya-ku, Tokyo

Closest station: Ebisu

Hours 11 a.m.–5 a.m.

Open every day

This ramen-ya is famous for its Cheese Miso Tonkotsu Ramen. A special type of local artisan cheese called Golden Gouda is incorporated into the soup and also piled high on top. It's shaved to almost a powder form right at the bar, so it sinks and melts into the soup to give you a rich, thick, satisfying meal. You won't be hungry for an hour or five later.

Usagi Shokudo, Master Mori-san

Aobadai 1-30-12 Meguro-ku, Tokyo

Closest station: Naka-Meguro

Open 11:30 a.m.–10 p.m.

Closed Mondays

They serve *tori paitan* here, which is ramen with a creamy chicken soup. There are only two menu items and they were out of one so we ordered the *torishiroramen*—their signature creamy chicken soup with a *shiodare*. There were delicate pieces of perfectly tender chicken and thin fried onions and shredded negi (Japanese green onion) on top with a crispy piece of garlic toast and some sweet minced garlic on the side. It was a graceful dish and very well-orchestrated. The restaurant is more upscale in a seated restaurant-style space. The line here took a little longer because of this but it was well worth the wait. They were voted best rookie tori paitan by *Tokyo Ramen of the Year* magazine in 2014, deservedly so.

Index

Page numbers in italics indicate photographs.

Acknowledgments

One of the last emails I received from my husband, Dave, the week my cookbook was due read: "I would be lying if I said I won't be happy when it's done!" Then he added, "Are we still having cheese ramen tonight?" and signed the note with a winking emoji. That pretty much sums up my life writing a cookbook.

My friends would say, "How do you do it all?" and the answer I would give them was "I don't. It's nuts." I gave up my marketing consulting business to devote myself to the cookbook and be at home for the kids. I found that when I took time out for myself, which I desperately needed on occasion, my family would get the short end of the stick because I'd have to make up the time working on recipes, instead of taking care of them. My daughter, Maggie, was initially excited to be my noodle maker but then she asked to be paid. I don't think my son, Ryan, washed his face the entire year because I was too busy to notice. And when asked at preschool do describe what I did, my daughter, Ellie, would say, "Sitting at the computer" and "Drinking juice (aka wine)." I gained ten pounds of ramen weight, but luckily, Dave told me he's never been into petite women. I turned "lunch with girlfriends" into "come over and try some of my ramen." So, we learned to adjust. I guess the answer to the question of how do I do it all is that I couldn't have done it without my village of friends who pitched in when I needed help and a super-supportive and forgiving family who always told me that the last ramen I served them was the best one they've had yet. Love you, guys, so much.

About the Author

Amy Kimoto-Kahn is a *yonsei*, a fourth-generation Japanese American, and a mom of three who lives in the San Francisco Bay Area. She is a graduate of the Miyajima Ramen School in Osaka, Japan, and has taught a popular series of Asian-inspired cooking classes for Williams-Sonoma. She shares her Japanese-American homestyle, kids-will-like-it-too recipes on her blog, *easypeasyjapanesey*. When she isn't cooking she runs a mom-focused marketing firm, Fat Duck Consulting, that she founded in 2008. You can visit her website at www.easypeasyjapanesey.com.